The 100 Best Movies Ever Made

...Mostly Suck

The 100 Best Movies Ever Made ...Mostly Suck

By Nigel S.
("Mr. Satanism")

INEPT
CONCEPTS

ISBN-13: 978-0615494623
ISBN-10: 0615494625

Printed in the United States of America. U.S.A.! U.S.A.!

Cover image © adimas/Fotolia. Used with permission.

Second Edition
(Less typos)

Those who can, do.

Those who can't, teach.

Those who can't do or teach
become movie critics.

Foreword

Fuck movies. Seriously, that's all people ever talk about: movies movies movies. If you're sitting around your place all bored, what do you do? You watch a movie. Going out on a date? Dinner and a movie. It's hardly ever dinner and a play, or dinner and skiing, or dinner and an armed robbery. It's always a goddamned movie. Do me a favor - next time you take your girl out, go hang gliding or manatee hunting or something. Try to show a little imagination once in a while.

Everybody wants to be in the movies too, and the people who aren't are way too interested in the people who are: "Did you hear what that movie star did?" Unless it's beyond freak show, who gives a shit? Now here you are reading a *book* about movies. Honestly, if it wasn't for movies people would get a lot more accomplished.

This book is about the "100 best movies ever made." You'll notice I put that in quotes, but I didn't do it because I'm one of those morons who thinks that you put things in quotes to emphasize them or whatever. You know, like the kind of illiterate, knuckle-dragging diphead who would make a sign that says something like this:

ALL LAPTOP'S "ON SALE"

or this:

"DELICIOUS" SANDWICHES

No, the reason I put "100 best movies ever made" in quotes is because I'm being ironic, like Alanis Morissette, whom I'm only bringing up because she just happens to be my laptop wallpaper as I write this and I can't stop staring at her jugs. I don't care what anyone says, I would hit that like a van full of uninsured Mexicans. I would hit that like your mom hits the bottle. I would hit that like that chunk of Skylab hit my Audi. When oh when will we share our forbidden love, Alanis? Stupid restraining order.

Where the hell was I? Oh yeah, movies. See, movie critics are always putting together these lists of the 100 best movies ever made, and even though each one is a *little* different they all generally pick the same boring shit over and over, which if you ask me makes the whole thing more than a little suspect. I mean really, do they honestly expect us to believe that there's not a single movie critic in the entire world who hates *The Graduate*? And how else do you explain the fact that kickass shit like *Vampires vs. Zombies* never appears on *any* of them? If you ask me, I think the clowns who come up with these lists are all secretly involved in a huge conspiracy to sell more copies of *Citizen Kane*.

That's why I decided this book was necessary (well, that and I'm behind on my mortgage). Lots of people like the idea of making a little project out of watching the 100 best movies ever made, because it's a good way to get some culture without actually going anywhere, doing anything, or changing their usual habits (i.e. sitting in front of the television every night and stuffing their face with sour cream & onion potato chips). The problem is that they usually find some list online or in a book or something and just start plowing through it, and by the time they get to the second or third flick with subtitles and/or *Annie Hall* they get frustrated and give up, not that I blame them.

That's where *The 100 Best Movies Ever Made ...Mostly Suck* comes in. Using complicated math, I combined all the "100 Best Movies" lists I could find into one super-ultimate list that includes movies from all over the world.[1] Even better, I tell you which ones are genuinely awesome, and which ones suck some serious. Armed with this information you can watch just the good ones, but still know enough about the rest to sound off at cocktail parties. Or, in your case, keggers. Let's not kid ourselves here.

So, movie fan, are you ready to save hundreds of hours of your life? Then turn the page! Or don't; if you've already paid for this book you can use it as a doorstop for all I care.

Disclaimer: Book may need to be taped to a brick to make an effective doorstop.

---

1   You'll notice that most of them are still American though, because our society may be collapsing and our chicks may be the fattest per capita, but we still make the best fucking movies on Earth. U.S.A.! U.S.A.!

Note: #101

I think when most people pick up a book like this the first thing they say to themselves is *I wonder what #101 was?* Well, according to my calculations, *Day for Night* (1973) is the 101st best movie ever made. Ha ha! Better luck next time, sucker! Actually, as it turns out, the guy who made *Day for Night*, François Truffaut, is an actor in movie #100, so I guess he back-doored his way in here after all. The devious frog bastard.

The 100 Best Movies Ever Made
...Mostly Suck

#100

Close Encounters of the Third Kind

(1977)

Science Fiction

Being #100 on a list of the 100 best anything kinda sucks. It's like being second in line at a gang bang. This flick is actually pretty good though, and it's filled with classic scenes, like the mashed potatoes scene, and the "dancing mailboxes" scene, and the scene where the main guy builds a mountain out of garbage in his living room, and, uh... Okay, fine, so maybe the scenes are ridiculous, but you have to understand that this movie was made in the 1970's and believe it or not it totally captures the flaky, hippie, New-Agey attitude people back then had towards UFOs and being alien-abducted. It really was a more innocent time. Nowadays, it's all about being probed.

One place *Close Encounters* does screw up is when it says that all this shit is going down in the "present day." Let's face it, even goofy-ass white guys like the main cat in this movie don't call people "turkey" anymore. I mean, there's no disco dancing or anything, but it's obviously the 1970's. They probably

3

should've done a little more research, because then they would have known that it wouldn't be the 1970's forever and sooner or later expecting people to buy that this is happening in the "present day" would be completely ridiculous. It's sort of the inverse to my rule about making sci-fi movies happen far enough in the future that you won't be around by the time everything you predicted turns out to be hilariously wrong. Take a look in the mirror right now. Unless you plan on wearing THAT outfit twenty years from now, never say your movie is happening in the present day.

So, the gist of the story is that all these jokers are being alien-abducted, except for a few who just get a memo to meet the aliens later, which is where the whole plot kinda falls apart. The main guy, for example, spends most of the movie trying to get to where the aliens are and dealing with endless grief along the way when the little pricks could've just picked him up any old time they wanted to. For Christ's sake, their UFO pulls up right behind his truck in one part! In fact, the vast majority of the folks the aliens invite never even make it to the party, all because the fickle bastards couldn't be bothered to give them a lift. What, were they afraid someone else would call shotgun or change the radio station or something? Nice priorities, aliens.

And what is with the slovenly, white trash broad whose kid gets abducted? If I was her I'd be ecstatic to be rid of that little wiener, but she's so upset you'd think somebody stole her stash or her alimony check got lost in the mail or something. In fact, you know what would've worked out way better for everybody? If the aliens took the main guy's three out-of-control brats

4

instead. Then instead of going into outer space at the end he could've stayed behind and made some new ones with that sexy-ass wife of his. I'd take a roll in the hay with her over the wonders of the universe any day.

Suggested Alternative: *Repo Man* (1984).

#99

Stagecoach

(1939)
Western

"Walter *Wanger* Presents"??? Ha ha ha! "Wanger."

Okay, this is technically a western, but in practice it's more like one of those stupid *Airport* movies from the 1970's. All the *Airport* movies were basically the same – various goofballs are traveling from point A to point B when a calamity occurs – and this flick follows that pattern exactly. The goofballs in this particular case are: the local sheriff; the stagecoach driver (who sounds like he's still going through puberty); a salesman; a drunk doctor; a pregnant chick who's nine months in but still looks completely doable; a gambler (played by that one guy who's always in old movies); a Republican; and a blonde who everybody else hates so I assume she's the town Jew. Oh, and they also pick up John Wayne along the way.

As for the calamity, this time it's the threat of an Indian attack, followed (a long eventually later) by the actual Indian attack. Naturally everyone's got their own little sideplot full of drama going on (the Republican stole some money, one of the dames is worried about her husband, John Wayne is jonesing to shoot some fools, etc.), and naturally the pregnant broad drops kid right in the middle of everything. It's all so fucking predictable. All they left out was the little girl who needs a heart transplant and the part where the pilot dies and one of the passengers has to land the stagecoach before they run out of fuel.

For real, can someone please explain to me how this is better than any other old-timey western? Even for the 1930's it's fairly corny, there's way too much (non) comedic relief (if I was in this movie, I would've killed that goofy fucking stagecoach driver myself), and let's not forget the part where some dame we never saw before and never see again shows up just so she can sing a song for absolutely no reason. Way to bring the movie to a grinding fucking halt. And then there's the shit no one wants to see, like people bickering (if I enjoyed that, I'd still be married), and watching someone down so much booze and coffee that they puke (ditto, except in my ex-wife's case throw in Abilify too). Besides, I can't stand John Wayne. He acts like a dick in almost all his movies, and that fucking drawl he's got going on? Before he got popular, we used to call people who talked like that "retarded." Seriously, fuck John Wayne. And fuck this movie.

Suggested Alternative: *The Big Bus* (1976)

#98

Raiders of the Lost Ark

(1981)

Adventure

Nowadays this flick is known as *Indiana Jones and the Raiders of the Lost Ark*, like they're afraid people are too goddamned stupid to remember that it's an Indiana Jones movie or something. I would love to know who thought that was really necessary. You don't see them changing the names of all the James Bond movies to *James Bond and Dr. No*, or *James Bond and the Moonraker*, do you? Seriously, talk about condescending.

That bullshit aside, here's one movie that definitely deserves to be on this list. It's got people impaled on spikes, killed with poisoned darts, shot, set on fire, scarred for life when they pick up a red-hot medallion (later this guy gets melted by God, so I suppose in the long run a hand injury is the least of his problems), exploded, machine-gunned, chopped up in airplane propellers, tossed out of moving vehicles, thrown through windshields, driven off cliffs, run over by trucks, and disintegrated. And it was an especially savvy move making most of the bad guys Nazis, but the main bad guy French.

Nazis aren't exactly the most popular cats around, but *nobody* likes the French.

There's so much awesome going on that you can easily ignore the minor fuckups, like the TV antennas in 1936 Cairo, or the fact that the Nazi who gets control of the truck during the big car chase could've ended things right then and there if he'd just pulled off to the side of the road. Not to mention the total lack of tits. Speaking of tits, I was never all that impressed with Indiana Jones's girl, but if you can believe her PMS-fueled rant when he first tracks her down he bagged that when it was well below the limit, so kudos to him. If that's how he rolls he really needs to nail that chick in the class he teaches who took the time to write "love you" on her eyelids. Actually, scratch that. He's teaching at the college level so she's probably too old for him.

They made a few sequels to this movie, each one half as good as the last. There was also a TV show (they went the "Jim Henson's Indiana Jones Babies" route), some corny novels (I believe one of them had vampires in it), and a hopelessly shitty Marvel comic book. In other words, there's a reason why no one ever organizes an Indiana Jones convention.

Suggested Alternative: *The Mummy* (1999)

#97

The Third Man

(1949)
Mystery

The big quotable line from this flick is "I was a friend of Harry Lime." Yeah, I know, kinda lame, but it beats being a friend of Dorothy.

It all starts when this cat finds out that his buddy got run over by a truck. After the funeral the cops tell him that it's no great loss because the dude was the biggest crook around, but the main guy isn't buying it so he starts snooping around and before long people are chasing him down any street that has poor lighting because, you know, *film noir*. The big twist comes when it turns out that the buddy is actually alive (spoiler warning), but most people will have already figured that out, especially if they have the "Criterion Collection" DVD because the stupid assholes give it away on the goddamned cover. (Besides, the buddy is played by that guy who's super famous for doing the *War of the Worlds* hoax and flipping out over some frozen peas, and his name is right there in the beginning credits. When the best-known actor in the movie hasn't shown up by the halfway point I think most folks are gonna put two and two together.)

The major problem with this flick is that the story hinges almost entirely on people being complete idiots. Seriously, there's no reason why the main guy should've thought that there was a mystery to investigate in the first place; he only gets suspicious because someone tells him that there were three people creeping around when his buddy bought the bucket, but the buddy's cronies insist that there were only two. If they had just said something like "Oh yeah, come to think of it there was another guy. I think his name was Carl," then that would've been the end of it right there. But no, they have to act as suspicious and mysterious as possible. Way to play it cool, morons.

Of course the main guy isn't exactly Copernicus either. Even after people start getting murdered he's still doing stupid shit like climbing into mysterious cars with complete strangers and calling sketchy characters out on deserted streets where there's no witnesses. At least there's an okay chase through the sewers at the end, but frankly even that scene could've used some more gunplay or maybe a few giant ants. Really the best thing about this flick is the Czechoslovakian babe who's mixed up in the whole thing; you'd better believe I'd sign up for some of that. Czech please! It's kind of a ruthless move on the main guy's part to be sniffing around right after he shoots her boyfriend though.

Suggested Alternative: *Kiss Me Deadly* (1955)

```
■□■□■□■□■□
```

#96

```
■□■□■□■□■□
```

The Philadelphia Story

(1940)
Comedy

Katharine "Kat" Hepburn was a huge sex symbol back in the day, but frankly I always thought she looked like a man. She definitely doesn't hold a candle to the great screen presences of the modern era, like Misty Mundae or that girl who fucked the dead guy in *Clerks* (1994). Hell, even compared to the other dames in this movie she comes up short; the secondary chick is way hotter, and even the mouthy little girl looks like she has more potential. How hilarious would it have been to look Katharine Hepburn right in the eye and tell her that you'd rather wait four years for her co-star to be legal? I'll bet she would've had a coronary.

So, this joker wants to get revenge on Katharine Hepburn for being his ex-wife, so he crashes her second-tier celebrity wedding with some undercover paparazzi who want to get the scoop. Katharine Hepburn figures his idiot scheme out immediately though, so her ex switches to his backup plan, socking her in the mouth. Oh, wait, my mistake - the backup plan is actually blackmail. (Apparently he did dish out a few drunken beat-downs back when they were married, but it's okay because judging by everyone's reaction they were the hilarious kind.) Everyone's an utter cock to each other for a while and it's all fairly entertaining, but just like in real life things don't get really interesting until they add booze to the mix. Pretty soon Katharine Hepburn is soused and throwing herself at one of the reporters in front of everybody, which leads to the best line in the movie when she makes her entrance the next morning and her uncle says "What ho, the bride!" See, it's like a double meaning.

The wrap-up is full-on retarded though: the ex-husband and the reporter *both* ask Katherine Hepburn to marry them, but the loser doesn't even blink when she makes her choice. "Yeah, you're the love of my life, or not, either way. I call Best Man." And don't even get me started on the reporter's girlfriend - she just *stands there* while he proposes to another broad right in front of her! Nice spine, bitch; could I maybe borrow it sometime to snake my drain? Seriously, it really needs it - I think somebody ran a kitten through the garbage disposal or something.

This flick does have a few good points: there's enough cruelty for three family Thanksgivings; the actor playing the reporter plays a good drunk (it's not all about falling down and slurring, community theater dipshits; take a lesson from this cat); the precocious little girl is actually funny instead of infuriating; and the reporter's girl is cute *and* a doormat, which is one of my favorite combinations. Overall though the story is just too ridiculous, and it's impossible to buy three different cats all panting after the same drag queen-looking broad. Heh. How hilarious would it have been to look Katharine Hepburn right in the eye and tell her that you mistook her for a drag queen? I'll bet she would've stabbed you.

Suggested Alternatives: *The Phenix City Story* (1955), *A Christmas Story* (1983) or *The Story of O* (1975)

#95

Butch Cassidy and the Sundance Kid

(1969)

Western

Remember that episode of *The Brady Bunch* where one of the kids got all obsessed with Jesse James so his parents tracked down a cat who actually got robbed by the dude (by raising him from the dead, I assume) and he explains that Jesse James was, in fact, a huge cocksucker? And then the kid has a dream where Jesse James shows up and sexually assaults Jan and Marcia over and over and over again? Or maybe I had that dream. Irregardless, if there's one (other) thing I took away from that episode, it's that the whole concept of the "honorable thief" is a total myth that only exists in crappy novels and bullshit movies like this. If you're one of those morons who just can't get over the idea though, that's fine by me. Drop me a line at the e-mail address elsewhere in this book and we'll set up a time when I can ransack your apartment.

As endearing as Butch Sundance and the Rawhide Kid's crime spree is, eventually some bounty hunters do come after them, and that's when this flick comes to such a complete and sudden halt that Newton's first law is pretty much out the window. Tough break, Isaac. For real, the next half hour or so is just one long, boring chase (more of a slog, actually) where *nothing fucking happens.* Have you ever had one of those dreams where a monster is after you but your feet are stuck in mud or something and you can't get away? This chase is kind of like that, except without the suspense. Eventually Butch and the Two-Gun Kid realize that this scene is never gonna end unless they get the hell out of ~~Dodge~~ wherever they are, so they decide to hit the road incognito, along with Kid Colt's girl, who's 26, single, and a teacher. Or, as she puts it, "the bottom of the pit." Ha! A hundred years later and things haven't really changed, have they, ladies? Sorry, but it's true.

So first these clowns go to New York, where we see everything they do via tinted, old-timey photographs (too cheap to shoot on location, I see), but eventually they end up in Bolivia, where... Okay, hold the mayo. Once a movie relocates the entire principal cast to fucking *Bolivia* can you still call it a western? What if they all decided to go to Antarctica next? Or the moon? Hey, I think it's a pretty good question.

Irregardless, once they get to Boliva they decide to rob a bank in Spanish, somehow forgetting that there's only two of them and two grown men can barely carry enough Bolivian money to buy lunch, much less make it worth all the trouble they're going through. Seriously, four jobs later they've cleared just enough to risk ordering two rounds of drinks and a pineapple, and they have to send back the pineapple. It's a matter of principle though, so eventually the locals get fed up with their gringo horseshit and the Bolivian army shows up and blows their asses away. I guess we're supposed to feel bad during this part, but good riddance, I say. At least now there won't be a sequel.

Oh wait, there was a sequel. Goddammit.

Suggested Alternative: *El Topo* (1970)

#94

Jaws

(1976)
Thriller

Jaws is about three dudes – a tough guy, a smart guy, and an emotional guy – who kill a big shark that's been eating the shit out of everybody. Actually, the shark manages to eat the tough guy too, and the smart guy ends up hiding behind a big rock until it's all over (See? Smart.), so I guess *Jaws* is really about an emotional guy who kills a big shark etc.

Either way, when this movie first came out it made so damn much money that everyone involved still has enough bread to buy a brand new car whenever it rains so they don't have to go through all the trouble of rolling their windows up. It also invented the whole concept of the "summer blockbuster," so next time you sit through a piece of dripping shit like *Armageddon* (1998) or *Wild Wild West* (1999), you can pretty much blame *Jaws*.

Since the shark explodes at the end (spoiler warning) you'd think it would be pretty hard to come up with a non-retarded idea for a sequel (they didn't even have the good sense to set one up by showing a bunch of shark eggs secreted away somewhere at the end), but that never stopped Hollywood before so eventually they made *Jaws 2* (1978), *Jaws 3-D* (1983), **and** *Jaws: The Revenge* (1987). Some con artists even made *Jaws 5* (1995) and *Jaws in Japan* (2010). They also puked up novelizations of Parts 2 & 4 (which are actually better than the movies, even though one of them blames the shark on voodoo), a Jaws game, a *Jaws 2* comic book, a Jaws ride, and three awful Jaws video games - one for the ZX Spectrum 8-bit home computer, one for Nintendo, and one for Playstation 2 and Xbox. Ironically, that last one is by far the lousiest.

On top of all that there were assloads of rip-offs starring every possible animal that lives in the ocean – giant octopuses, barracudas, killer whales, other sharks, salt water crocodiles, and even flying fucking piranhas – almost all of which steal as much shit from *Jaws* as legally possible. Favorite bits to swipe include a guy in charge who won't close the beaches, the part where a bunch of drunken cornheads try to kill the monster, and that famous poster of Jaws zeroing in on the hapless chick like me zeroing in on a girl with low self-esteem. One flick, *Great White* (1981), stole so much from *Jaws* that the Jaws people sued their dicks off and now Steven Spielberg keeps the dicks in a jar in his office. If you ever take a meeting with Spielberg, ask to see them.

In short, the only way *Jaws* could've been any more popular is if it also starred C-3PO and Princess Leia, and after the credits one of them blew you. This doesn't mean that *Jaws* is perfect though. In fact, there's three major *Jaws* Flaws:

1) Considering the fact that a large portion of this story takes place at the beach, almost no time is spent lingering over sexy bikini babes. In fact, the only notable hottie in the entire movie (the girl who warns everybody that Jaws is in the tide pool) is sporting jeans, a t-shirt, and an Aunt Jemima doo-rag. She pulls it off, but she would've looked way better in a two-piece. Or nothing.

2) Five people and a medium-sized dog? That's it? For a shark to come across as truly badass, he needs to be a lot more hungry than that.

3) And, finally, the number one problem with *Jaws*: "Jaws" is a really stupid name for a movie. I know it was a book first, but "Jaws" is a stupid name for a book too, so I'm sorry, but that's no excuse.

Suggested Alternative: *Grizzly* (1976)

🎞️🎞️

#93

🎞️🎞️

Wild Strawberries

(1957)

Drama

Now this is the kind of shit that gives the 100 Best Movies Ever Made a bad name. Drive, drive, drive, talk, talk, talk. Why is it that the flicks with subtitles are always the ones with the most talking? If that's the way you want to play it, just mail me the fucking script. Then I can read it on the john and kill two birds with one kidney stone. Honestly, would it really be that hard to dub this into English like they do Godzilla movies? *"Oh my God you can't do that, the words won't match their lips!"* Who gives a shit? If you're so great at reading lips, I say you could probably get through most movies without the sound, much less subtitles. Japanese cartoons might be a bit of a problem, but half the time those have subtitles too, as if cartoon characters' mouths are animated to such minute perfection that you can tell what language they're speaking in anyway. Don't point this out to someone who gets off on them though, because believe me, you will *never* hear the end of it. God I hate people who are into Japanese cartoons. Except of course the sexy chicks who dress up as their favorite characters. They rock.

Wild Strawberries is about this old geezer who takes a road trip to some university because they're gonna give him an honorary degree. The story isn't really about the degree though, it's more about how much the old goat regrets everything, like not being able to pork his own cousin,[2] and the fact that his wife was a goddamned whore. Along the way he also has some nightmares, including that one where it's exam day and you haven't been to class all semester and never even bought the book. Or maybe that was a flashback, which would explain why he's getting an honorary degree and not a real one. He also picks up some hitchhikers, one of whom is a hot little blonde who, unfortunately, never shows us her tits. What the fuck? This *is* a Swedish movie, and the Swedish *are* perverts, right? They sure picked a lousy time to rein it in. And if the actress had popped 'em out and then **regretted** it later, think how symbolic and meta *that* would've been. Talk about a missed opportunity.

Anyway, this movie is completely boring and pointless, although I suppose you might learn something about regret because at the very least you'll regret watching it. If you really want to understand regret though, I recommend getting blackout drunk every morning for the next month, whether you have something important to do that day or not. Then dry out and see what happens.

Suggested Alternative: *Going in Style* (1979)

---

2   Fucking degenerate. In his defense though, she is kind of cute.

#92

My Fair Lady

(1964)
Musical

Two jokers make a bet that they can turn one of those annoying twats who hock flowers at the club around last call into a dame classy enough to take to the track. The broad they pick is legendary hottie Audrey Hepburn, and I guess she really was a great actress because even though she's one of the standout babes of all time her character is so obnoxious that even I wouldn't fuck her, and I've been known to hang around reality show shoots and pick up the leftovers. Imagine if Rodney Dangerfield's part in *Caddyshack* (1980) was played by a hot chick and you'll get the general idea. Hell, even the main guy gets so irritated with her that at various points he threatens to throw her out a window, beat her with a broomstick, and worse. Finally, someone who knows how to talk to women.

Since teaching someone to have manners and talk good isn't very interesting to watch, they employ all these gimmicks in a (failed) attempt to make it less boring. Too bad the vast majority of these make zero sense whatsoever. For example, in one part Audrey is supposed to watch this flame in a mirror because it flares up when she pronounces shit right (yeah, I know: duh), but the mirror's spinning around and around for absolutely no reason, which looks cool but would make actually seeing something in it next to impossible. Honestly, Rube Goldberg wouldn't sign off on this shit.

This nonsense just goes on and on and Audrey doesn't get it and she doesn't get it and she doesn't get it until suddenly in one fell swoop she goes from still not getting it to understanding perfectly in like two seconds. In movie-speak, this is called "the moment of clarity," or, "lazy writing." Irregardless, now she's money so they take her to the ball where she totally bamboozles the Queen of Vampires into thinking she's royalty, which means that the main guy wins the bet. The end.

Oh, wait, apparently there's more (ugh). Audrey suddenly realizes that she was just a pawn in all of this (I guess you can lead a whore to water, but you can't make her think), so she gets all pissy and runs off. She doesn't really have any place to go, but fortunately for her she's picked up a stalker along the way who's more than willing to help her out. It looks like it's curtains for her weird, non-sexual, emotionally abusive relationship with the main guy, until someone realized that this damn movie was closing in on the three-hour mark so they just had her come back without too much of a fuss so that the cast and crew could go home and actually spend some time with their families.

As you can see, the story is pretty lame (putting Audrey in a bikini or a Catholic schoolgirl uniform would have helped things out considerably; too bad they didn't think of that), but in the end the only real way to judge a musical is by the songs, since most people will be exposed to the songs way more often than they'll sit through the whole movie. Think about it, how many times have you actually seen the movie *Footloose* (1984) in its entirety? Incidentally, if it's more than twice, congratulations. You're gay.

So how are the songs in this flick? Well, they're great in theory: half of them are about shit like avoiding work, how irrational women are, and petty revenge, and there's no way the "I Could Have Danced" one is about anything but fucking:

I could have danced all night!
And still have begged for more.
I could have spread my wings
And done a thousand things I've never done before.

I'm with you, Audrey. Let's start with anal and we'll work our way through the *Kama Sutra* from there. Where was I? Oh yeah, the songs. Sad to say, only one of them is particularly memorable, and it's about, ugh, getting married. Sorry, but one good song does not a musical make. Should've hired Elvis Costello, idiots.

Suggested Alternative: *Trading Places* (1983)

#91

Le Million

(1931)
Comedy

This frog artist is stone cold broke, but at least he has plenty of hot ass hanging around. I wonder how he manages to... Oh, that's right, French chicks aren't total gold-digging tramps like American ones.

Still, it's looking pretty bleak for our main guy – even the butcher is screaming for his pound of flesh (Ha! Get it?) – but it seems like his luck has finally changed when he wins the lottery. Too bad the ticket's in his jacket and one of his tricks gave the jacket to some weirdo. Of course the jacket keeps changing hands in unlikely ways, and of course everyone runs all over town looking for it, and of course zany shenanigans ensue. You know, movie critics always beat the shit out of flicks like *Rat Race* (2001) and *Cannonball Run III* (1989), where it's just a bunch of hack actors chasing each other around and engaging in madcap antics, but make the movie old and the hack actors French and suddenly it's one of the best movies ever made. Fucking hypocrites.

Even worse, for a wild & crazy movie this really isn't very wild & crazy, even by 1930's standards. And back then just walking outside without your hat was considered mildly outrageous. There are plenty of parts where random people suddenly start singing, though. Not enough to really count as a musical, but enough to be weird and kind of distracting. I mean, I can see bursting into song if you just found out that you won a million frog dollars, but during your Fight Club anarchist meeting? Give me a fucking break.

They did get one thing right though: the chicks. The surrender-monkey chippies in this flick are just amazingly fine. If you ask me, it's high time 1930's hairstyles made a comeback. In fact, I almost started to get into the whole thing when the main guy said that his fiancee, the finest piece in the movie by far, was a dancer. But then I remembered that back then "dancer" wasn't code for "coked-up stripper." As it turns out she's actually a ballerina, which is still hot, but nowhere near as hot as how I pictured her when I was in the shower later.

Incidentally, considering the fact that the main guy has a fiancee *and* is carrying on with some trick on the side, this flick passes up way too many opportunities for a sexy French catfight between the two. I mean, they cross paths multiple times and they both know the score, but all they do is glare at each other. Come on - give us we want and start swinging, bitches.

Suggested Alternative: Any comedy where college students go on a scavenger hunt

#90

Brief Encounter

(1945)
Drama

It's a scientific fact that stolen food tastes better, stolen liquor gets you drunker, and stolen ass is the sweetest ass of all. Unfortunately, most affairs involve one ugly person cheating on another ugly person with a third person who's just as ugly as the other two, while a fourth ugly person takes notes so she can keep her story straight when she calls *Jerry Springer*. So why do people do it? Guys will tell you that it's for the sex (duh), but most chicks say that, for them, cheating fills an emotional need, and the sex itself isn't important at all. This illustrates one of the biggest differences between men and women: women can find a way to justify anything.

As you might have guessed, this flick is about two people cheating, but it was made in the 1940's which means that it's so damn pussified that they never even get around to screwing! That's no great loss for us though, because the broad is kinda ugly, not to mention completely boring: her entire life consists of watching her husband do crossword puzzles, going to the movies once a week, and hanging around train stations like the two-bit tramp she turns out to be. The guy she steps out with, meanwhile, is a doctor, and frankly I'm a little appalled that he would put all this effort into stealing another man's sub-standard wife when he could have his pick of sub-standard nurses, plenty of whom are actually available because they got into the profession solely to meet a doctor in the first place, only to realize too late that doctors don't actually marry sub-standard nurses. Doctors marry slightly over-the-hill models, and then cheat on them with 22-year-old drug company reps. If you ever wondered why most nurses are so grumpy, now you know.

So anyway, the floozy in this flick covers her tracks by coming up with all these extensive, complicated lies when simple lies (or just not saying anything) would do, but it hardly matters since a) her chump husband doesn't even have a clue, and b) nothing worth covering up really happens anyway. Sure, the doctor shoves his tongue down her throat once or twice, but I've gone further than that with my own cousin plenty of times, and once with a chick we thought was my long-lost sister but who turned out to be a con artist trying to swindle us. In fact, the worst thing that comes of the whole deal is the doctor's buddy telling him that he's onto them and they can't use his flat anymore because he doesn't want jizz all over the place. Compare that to what could've happened to them if this story took place in the Middle East and you'll start to realize just how lame this movie really is.

Suggested Alternative: Turn on Lifetime. If what you're looking at isn't a sexier version of this, wait thirty minutes.

#89

Network

(1976)
Drama

The only thing most people remember about this movie is that a nightly news guy cracks up on the air and yells "I'm as mad as hell, and I'm not gonna take this any more!" Me, I remember it more for being this weird stepping stone between really old shit and relatively new shit. I mean, the cop from *Kiss Me Deadly* (1955) is in it, but so is the housekeeper from *Two and a Half Men* (2003-2011)! Yeah, she was pretty fat back then, too.

Watching someone have a complete mental and emotional breakdown is way more entertaining if you're actually there to egg them on (remind me to tell you about my second wife sometime), so fortunately there is a little more to the story, but in the end the main gist of it is that television is degenerate and stupid. Of course most people figured that out when they saw their first episode of *Small Wonder, What a Dummy,* or *Family Guy,* so it's not like it's this big revelation or anything. In fact, parts of this movie are as dumb as any of those shows, like the scene where the main guy tells his wife that he's leaving her for a younger piece in this goofy-ass, flip manner that would have most chicks shooting first and asking questions later. She just stands there taking it all in though, because if she screamed at him like a normal person would we might miss some of his "witty" dialogue.

Of course the crazy newscaster ends up with his own show (so ironic!), and naturally it's smash hit that trounces everything else on television. Except, the narrator informs us, *The Six Million Dollar Man*, *All in the Family*, and *Phyllis*. As you can see, the bar was set pretty high back in 1976. I mean, *Phyllis*. Eventually though his ratings start to tank, so what do they do? They have him assassinated! (Spoiler warning.)

Okay, seriously, do they really expect us to buy this shit? I know they set up a bunch of complicated malarkey explaining why they can't just fire the screwball, but there's plenty of ways to get a TV show canceled: change the time slot every other week, put it up against the biggest hit running (in this case I guess that would be *Phyllis*), show all the episodes out of order, add seven lady truckers to the cast... The list goes on and on. Why would these clowns risk getting busted for first-degree murder when they could achieve the exact same thing by introducing a lovable, wisecracking robot? Long story short, this flick is utterly ridiculous.

It did give us the phrase "impugn a man's cockmanship" though, so I guess that's something.

Suggested Alternative: *Videodrome* (1983)

```
□□□□□□□
```

#88

```
□□□□□□□
```

La Terra Trema
(1948)
Drama

Someone told me that this movie was about Greek people, but it turns out it's about Sicilian people. That thoroughly sucks. I had a really funny joke about *King Frat* (1979) that I wanted to lead with.

The story begins with a bunch of fishermen complaining that they do all the work, but the cats who sell the fish make all the money. The solution seems simple enough to me: be one of the cats who sells the fish. I can hear the fishermen's argument already though: "My father was a fisherman and his father was a fisherman and his father before him was a fisherman and his father before him we're not sure about but he was probably a fisherman and if he wasn't he wanted to be!" So what? My father, his father, and his father before him were all gay (seriously, I'm lucky to be here); that doesn't mean I have to chug pole too.

At least the main guy doesn't subscribe to this lazy, quitter philosophy. Instead of just sitting around on his dick, he starts a riot and then rounds up some of his cronies and they do indeed go into business for themselves. Unfortunately, the main guy does have one thing in common with his forefathers: he's a goddamned idiot. He ends up wrecking his boat, gets ripped off when he sells the anchovies they did manage to catch,[3] and eventually even his girl gets fed up with his incompetence and takes off on him. Seems like things can't get much worse for this fool, unless he gets eaten by a school of flying piranhas and there's still an hour left in this movie so I'm not entirely ruling that out.

So an entire month goes by, and the whole family's starving. (You know, if you live right next to the ocean and are starving to death, maybe "fishing" isn't exactly your strongest skill set.) If you've ever been poor, you know what happens next: one son joins a gang, one of the daughters starts swapping her ass for junk jewelry (before you judge, take it from me, she's lucky to be getting that), and finally they all get evicted. The main guy, meanwhile, spends all his time drinking and fighting (like a girl, but fighting nonetheless), but finally he drags himself out of the gutter long enough to go crawling back to the fishmongers for a job and the movie ends with his spirit completely broken and everyone else worse off than they were before.

Moral: Never try.

Suggested Alternative: *Earthquake* (1974)

---

3   What did he expect? People hate anchovies. They should've thrown those back immediately and tried to catch some pepperoni fish.

#87

Tootsie

(1982)
Comedy

You know that old adage "The more things change, the more they stay the same"? It's one of those stupid sayings that doesn't actually make any sense when you stop to think about it, but it totally applies here: men dressing up like women isn't funny now (examples: *Big Momma's House 3*, your brother-in-law), and it wasn't funny then (example: this piece of shit). Before I watched even one second of this movie I made three predictions:

1) There will be no actual jokes, because they will assume that just seeing a man dressed as a woman is endlessly hilarious. Check.

2) There will be a hopelessly oblivious dude who macks all over the Female who's Actually a Guy (F.A.G.) and won't take no for an answer. I was actually wrong about this one. There are *two* hopelessly oblivious dudes in the movie who do this.

3) The F.A.G. will want to get with some chick, but he can't because if he does she'll find out the truth. Wrong

again. There are *two* chicks in this flick that he wants to get with, etc.

I haven't seen an episode of *Bosom Buddies* since the 1980's so there were a couple I forgot, like the part where a bunch of clueless women get naked and/or scantily clad around the F.A.G. and he's "hilariously" flustered, or the bit where zany coincidences involving the F.A.G. and his F.A.G. activities lead one or more people to suspect that he's gay. This lazy-ass script didn't miss a beat though. It's like the winner in a contest for the most obvious movie ever.

For real, this flick is FUCKING HORRIBLE; it's just a bunch of sitcom bullshit. So many awesome, classic comedies came out in the 1980's – *Vacation* (1983), *Ghostbusters* (1984), *Stripes* (1981), *Back to School* (1986), *Caddyshack* (1980), *Evil Dead II* (1987) – and this by-the-numbers, hack-ridden, seen-it-all-a-million-times-before-and-it-sucked-then-too crap makes the top 100 list??? I mean, the theme song *actually* has lines that go like this:

Go, Tootsie, go,
Roll, baby, roll,
Sweet Tootsie roll

For fuck's sake. I could write wittier shit if I was in a coma. (Incidentally, the Briar & Associates Collections Group of Greater Dubuque thinks that I am, so if anyone asks, this book was ghostwritten by Stephen King.)

And let's look at this movie from a chick's point of view. Ladies, can you think of *anything* creepier than the part where the F.A.G. is in bed with this girl he wants to fuck, who thinks he's a broad, and he starts stroking her hair while she falls asleep? And what about the other gal in this movie? The F.A.G. nails her, then blows her off, lies to her, tells her he's in love with a less-attractive chick, and, finally, tops it all off by completely humiliating her on multiple, complex levels that will require years of therapy to even begin to sort out. We never find out what ultimately happens to her, but my guess is that she becomes a drug-addled, half-hearted lesbian who, years later, is found hanging from a noose in a fleabag motel with a paperback copy of *He's Just Not That Into You* still clutched in her withered, track-marked arms.

The main guy in *Tootsie* is such an asshole.

Suggested Alternative: Stop sucking cock

□□□□□□□□

#86

□□□□□□□□

Doctor Zhivago

(1965)

Drama

Wow, a doctor *and* a rock-star poet? This Zhivago cat is a regular Buckaroo Banzai. Well, except that Buckaroo Banzai didn't sleepwalk through history primarily concerned with how much tail he can score behind his wife's back.

It all starts in the olden days, with Dr. Z and his rich friends living the good life while Russian hippies protest in the streets and occasionally get their heads bashed in by the pigs. All is as it should be, until the Great World War I comes along and the hippies finally convince everyone to invent the Soviet Union, thus setting the stage for hundreds of shitty spy novels and *Rocky IV* (1985). Dr. Z is way too wishy-washy to pick sides (besides, how is that gonna get him laid?), but eventually he gets "drafted" by some counter-counter-revolutionaries and ends up in the thick of it anyway. That is, until he manages to desert while the rest of his unit is distracted by a bunch of shell-shocked women and children.

This cat is just full of admirable qualities.

To his credit he does make some effort to track down his family before he speed-dials the home office of the local escort service, but when he can't find them he shacks up with this chick he was previously banging on the side, who's not bad but frankly doesn't hold a bushka to his hot-ass, ex-czarist wife. Seriously, I'd hit that bourgeois bitch harder than a Soviet tank hits a student protestor. I guess I'm just a tsar fucker.

Besides the wife this flick does have a few other good elements, like people being shot and some low-key rioting, but mostly it's just Dr. Z wandering around being his own worst enemy for three fucking hours. Yeah, you read that right, *three hours*. As a general rule I hate really long movies like this (I'm a busy man, dammit), but to its credit at least this one has an intermission. Intermissions are cool because not only do they provide an opportunity for people to sneak in and see half a movie for free, but also because they give you time to hit the bathroom and rub one out. As Pee-Wee Herman learned the hard way, this is a lot smarter than just doing it right there in the theater. And he was watching a porno; can you imagine getting busted for something like that at a showing of *Doctor Zhivago*? Talk about embarrassing.

Suggested Alternatives: *Doctor Detroit* (1983), *Dr. No* (1962), *Dr. Butcher, M.D.* (1980)

```
□□□□□□□
```
#85
```
□□□□□□□
```

Rebel Without a Cause
(1955)
Drama

People can never discuss *Rebel Without a Cause* without bringing up the fact that the main actor in it only made three movies before he died. So what? The girl who played "Katya" in *Doctor Zhivago* only made one movie, and she's (probably) dead. Get a little perspective, idiots.

These old "youth runs wild" flicks are usually hopelessly lame ("Speeding again, Frankie? It's off to forestry camp with you!"), but this one isn't half bad, even by today's post-Columbine standards: these punks booze it up, get into knife fights at the planetarium, drive stolen cars over cliffs, kill puppies... One of them even takes a few pot shots at the pigs! Not too shabby.

For all the good times though it was still the 1950's, so the one thing nobody is allowed to do is land any tail. Sigmund "the Semen Monster" Freud would probably find that particularly interesting, because if you pay attention, *all* of the main kids' problems are *completely* sexual. For example, the main main kid is so sexually confused by the fact that his mom wears the cock in his family that he tries to choke his dad, and the main chick's pop throws a gasket whenever she looks too pretty or kisses him hello, a clear sign that he's working through a little post-incest guilt.

The most screwed-up of the lot though is the kid everybody calls "Plato" (because he's so goddamned stupid, I assume), who's obviously a gay queer. The part where he tries to pick up the main kid is especially embarrassing:

PLATO: "Hey you wanna come home with me? I mean there's nobody home at my house and heck, I'm not tired. Are you?... If you wanna come, we can talk and in the morning we can have breakfast..."

Embarrassing for him, I mean. For us, it's hilarious. Plato's big beef with his parents is that they aren't around at all, but they left him the house, a slave, and a gun, so I'd say he's got it pretty good. Hell, if it was the 1700's, he could vote.

Naturally it all ends in tragedy, but frankly I had a hard time giving a shit since everyone was such a goddamned crybaby. (Seriously, Plato, if you wiped some of the tears out of your eyes you might've actually hit one of those cops you shot at.) I think this flick would've been a lot more interesting if it was less about these whiners and their "big" problems and more about the peripheral punks and their day-to-day problems. Like coming up with knife money, for example. Think about it: you need a knife to rob somebody, but you need money to buy a knife. It's a total catch-22. Seeing how a high school dropout solved that conundrum would be way more entertaining than watching some tweaky little homo mack all over the cat from *East of Eden* (1955).

Suggested Alternative: *Suburbia* (1983)

#84

To Kill a Mockingbird

(1962)

Drama

This is a "coming of age" movie. Don't know what that is? Remember when you were 13 and your best friend's weird, college-age sister got you drunk on Uncle Oscars Popcorn Schnapps, let you feel her up, and then blew you? If someone had filmed that, it would be a coming of age movie. In more ways than one.

This movie is also a "courtroom drama." A courtroom drama is about someone who's on trial, usually for a crime they didn't commit. Also the person on trial is generally accused of something relatively serious, like murder or grand treason; you hardly ever see a courtroom drama set in, say, traffic court. The last half of any *Law & Order* (1990-2010) episode basically qualifies as a courtroom drama, except minus the drama because you know that the bad guy will always be found guilty, except during the first few seasons where sometimes they actually got away with it. Honestly, when it started out, *Law & Order* was actually kind of badass. Who wrote those later seasons anyway? The Comics Code Authority?

As you can see these are two completely different types of movies, and that's the main problem with this flick: it wants to be both at the same time. Sometimes mashing two different kinds of movies together can work (imagine if they mixed a Star Trek movie with a zombie movie, for example; that would be awesome), but when the two types of movies you pick are both completely boring, you need to come up with a pretty good gimmick or, not unlike that dead mockingbird, it just isn't gonna fly.

What they probably should've done is made one of the main kids the lawyer for the defense, sort of the legal equivalent of Doogie Howser or the Kid with the 200 I.Q. They didn't do that though. Instead, the two main kids come of age by watching a trial and seeing justice not be served, making this the movie equivalent of an *After School Special* where someone somehow learns a valuable lesson by watching Judge Judy engage in her obnoxious, twat antics on the television. And I really have to ask, why do all old courtroom movies take place in the summer in a building with no air conditioning? Is seeing people fan themselves supposed to add a bunch of suspense or something? *I sure hope that air conditioner repair guy gets there soon,* the writers probably imagine the audience thinking.

Getting back to this flick specifically, here's another good question: what is with the goofy-ass ending? After the trial is over the two main kids come of age even more when the neighborhood weirdo rescues them from a murderer while one of them is dressed as a ham. (One of the kids is dressed as the ham, I mean. I think it's important that I clarify that.) I'll admit that a plot to murder an underage ham would have added some excitement to this story, if it didn't undermine the seriousness of the situation to have one of the people involved dressed as giant ham in the first place.

As boring and ridiculous as it is, this flick did have a huge impact on pop culture. One of the kids actually invented the most annoying song of the 1980's when he says he's "walking like an Egyptian," and I'm pretty sure Boo Radley – one of the main characters in this flick – is who inspired your lamer black people to start calling each other "my boo."

Well, it was either him or Boo Berry.

Suggested Alternatives: *The Intruder* (1961)

#83

La Jour se Lève

(1939)
Drama

Okay, we've got a bunch of guys boozing on the job, macking all over everything in sight, manufacturing tons of drama over a chick they wouldn't even be interested in if someone else hadn't claimed her first... This movie is French all right.

The main frog already has his problems (the primary one, of course, being that he's French), but his troubles don't really begin until he starts bumping heads with some clown over, not one, but *two* pieces of ass, one of whom isn't even worth the effort. And the other one just barely. Even worse, the clown he gets into it with makes his living training little dogs to dance on stage and balance on balls and whatnot, and spends all his free time slinging bullshit, clumsily hitting on girls, and acting like a complete asshole. He's like the Dog Whisperer with no social filter. If that's your primary romantic rival, you need to take a long, hard look at yourself. And then drink some drain cleaner.

Fortunately the main frog comes up with a much better

solution - he kills the dog trainer. *Unfortunately,* he does this right in the middle of his own flat, and before long *le porcs* have the place surrounded. You can probably guess how it plays out from here, but remember, these are the rifle-dropping French, so it takes the cops the whole rest of this movie to finally bring the fool down.

It's hard to argue with anything that involves French people being shot, but I did have one serious problem with this flick: the subtitles. Apparently the joker pulling subtitle duty on the version I watched was a serious slack-ass, because he only bothered to translate the bare minimum needed to follow the plot. Folks will be talking and talking and talking with no accompanying subtitles and then suddenly they'll throw us a bone and translate one lousy sentence so we can just barely figure out what's going on. And I don't know about you, but if I hired someone for a gig that specifically involved "writing," I'd make damn sure that he didn't employ grocer's apostrophes and actually knew how to spell.

The weirdest thing about the subtitles though is that every once in a while a few lines are in a completely different font for no discernible reason. My guess is that the first subtitle guy did such a half-assed job that they had to bring someone else in to do some cleanup work, and he had some hang-up regarding the font his predecessor used so he insisted on picking another one. Seriously, what kind of OCD pinhead gets all riled up over a font? Duh. At any rate, it's all so sloppy and unprofessional that I can't help but wonder if they even got the basics of the story right. Hell, I don't speak a word of frog so for all I know this movie is actually about space aliens.

Suggested Alternative: *Targets* (1968)

#82

Fantasia
(1940)
Musical

I date a lot of single moms because it saves me a bundle (there's no cover charge to get into the gallery at family court), and whenever one of them asks me to bring over a Disney movie to distract her rugrats I always get this one. Because it's a timeless classic and one of the best movies ever made? Fuck no - because it's the one Disney cartoon every kid on earth is guaranteed to hate.[4] See, I know that before long they'll start to fidget, then they'll start acting up, and finally they'll get spanked and sent to bed early, which means I get into mom's pants that much sooner. Don't kids at least enjoy the Mickey Mouse part, you ask? I wouldn't know; I've never seen a little kid make it *to* the Mickey Mouse part. In fact, by that point mom and I are usually rounding third base.

Oh, and for extra laughs, later I always tell the little nose-pickers: "The only other Disney movie I like is *The Black Hole*, and I'm gonna be your daddy someday."

---

4   Well, okay, this and *The Three Caballeros* (1944).

The reason kids hate this cartoon is because there's no princesses or singing eels or even a Happy Meal tie-in: it's just a bunch of music videos, not one of which features Hannah Montana. *Music videos,* you ask? That's right, and it came out in 1940, so the next time you hear some baby boomer going on and on about how the hack-ass Beatles invented music videos you're completely justified if you punch him in the stomach and say "No, hippie, it was Walt Disney! Impeach Obama!" Sometimes I don't even wait for the subject to come up; sooner or later baby boomers try to bring *every* conversation around to the Beatles, so if you see a boomer start to open his mouth you might want to just go ahead and let him have it immediately. If it turns out he was just gonna ask where the bathroom is or order another gin & tonic you can always apologize later.

So, the first video is just a bunch of shapes and colors – yes, yes, I heard you: "I'm tripping!" Hilarious. Can we move on, please? – but the rest of them are a little more involved:

The Nutcracker Suite Fairies, flowers, bubbles, sparkles... One day I was walking down the street when suddenly this big gust of wind came along and blew a bunch of pink flower petals into the air and they flew all around me like a whirlwind. *Wow,* I thought at the time, *this is so gay.* The "Nutcracker Suite" sequence is a lot like that. Heh. "Nutcracker."

The Sorcerer's Apprentice Mickey Mouse is a wizard's "apprentice" (we all know what that means) who causes a bunch of water damage to his boss's castle. Despite popular conception no one actually likes Mickey Mouse, but he remains historically significant because he was the first major cartoon character based on a member of the disease-carrying vermin family, a trend that continues to this day in movies like *Secret of NIMH V: Plague of Vengeance.*

The Rite of Spring Hold on to your dicks, Christians (actually, maybe you'd better not - it might count as masturbation): in this section Disney advocates evolution. (I suppose now you'll be purging the house of every Uncle Scrooge comic and Little Mermaid makeup kit you can find, just like you did a few years ago when you found out they made a cartoon called *W.I.T.C.H.* You do know that's why your oldest ran away from home, don't you?) The best part of this one is when they get to the dinosaurs, because these aren't cutesy *Land Before Time Parts I-XXXVII* type dinosaurs; they're fairly realistic and pretty badass. I don't remember there ever being a theory that they all died out because of a "hot age" though. Maybe Al Gore's people snuck that in there.

Now might be a good time to take a leak, because the next part is just an ad pimping the soundtrack. Being 1940 and all I assume it was only available on 78's, reel-to-reels, or presented live by a traveling minstrel who would perform the entire movie for a shilling, a crust of bread, and a warm bed, and then rape your daughter and steal your horse – or possibly vice-versa – after everyone went to sleep. Hey, being entertained was hard in the olden days. Ask anyone. Next up:

The Pastoral Symphony This starts with some My Little

Pony-type unicorns running around, but fortunately it gets better. In fact, it all builds up to everyone getting loaded and fucking, and their drunken orgy is so out of control that the gods themselves show up to put a stop to it! There's even a part where we see some topless "mermaids" who actually turn out to be topless centaur chicks. It's a fake-out, but the good kind because I always liked the idea of centaur chicks way better than mermaids anyway. Think about it: you can't really fuck a mermaid, but the only thing preventing you from boning a centaur are your own sexual hang-ups. And you know what? I think this makes *Fantasia* the first movie in this book that actually has some tits in it! Well played, Walt.

Dance of the Hours Dancing ostriches and hippos. It fucking sucks. And did they really think we wouldn't notice that the music is the "Hello Muddah / Hello Fadduh / Here I am at / Camp Granada" song? Give me a fucking break.

Night on Bald Mountain This one is my favorite, mainly because I'm actually in it! It's fucking true - look for me about two minutes in, riding the horse. And let me tell you, the after-party they threw for the extras was something else. I woke up the next morning with my dick in one of the harpies.

So, it appears that at least three of these are definitely worth checking out. Years later they made a sequel, *Fantasia 2000*, but like *Blues Brothers 2000* and *Das Rheingold 2000: Robot Apocalypse*, it didn't go over so hot.

Suggested Alternative: *Pink Floyd: The Wall* (1982)

#81

Pather Panchali

(1955)
Drama

Christ, didn't we get enough of poor people suffering their destitute misery in that damn Sicilian fishing movie? It's all just a bunch of hypocrite bullshit anyway; if these filmmakers were really so concerned about the poor, they'd donate their money to charity instead of using it to make self-aggrandizing movies.

This flick is about an Indian family (7-11, not casino), and if nothing else it taught me that Indian people are just like everyone else: pathetic morons. This kind of threw me, because I'm a lifelong reverse racist and I always assumed that all Indian people were smarter than me. The family in this flick is a mess though: they're so fucking broke that they don't have two rupees to rub together, their goddamned house is falling down, their daughter's a klepto, they owe everybody money, and the dad spends all day talking about all the great scripts he's gonna write – someday – while sucking on a bong. Just like your brother-in-law!

Speaking of, there's also the inevitable freeloading in-law, an unbelievably irritating aunt who looks like a cross between a zombie, a bull dyke, and the Joker. It's too bad these people can't afford any stairs, because they really need to push her down some and put her out of everyone's misery. The old bag does kick the farm eventually, but it's not very satisfying. I wanted to see her taken down by jackals or something.

The amazing thing about life though is that things are never so bad that they can't get worse: the next thing you know, the *daughter* dies! Okay, really, I've had it. Who wants to spend two hours watching these miserable bastards suffer through their awful life? And there's two sequels! What could possibly happen to these poor hadji bastards next? Do they all get AIDS after being raped by the Devil?

Suggested Alternative: Not living in India

#80

The Sound of Music

(1965)
Musical

This flick gives me the perfect excuse to break out my favorite joke:

Q: What kind of pussy can you get in a convent?
A: Nun

Ha ha ha ha ha ha ha! Feel free to steal that if you want.

So, I saw this movie once before, on TV back in the 1970's (in the days before every TV had a remote control, it was a lot easier to just watch whatever came on than it was to get up and change the channel), but the only thing I really remembered about it was that eventually the Nazis came for everybody. This time, all I kept thinking was *Why couldn't they come sooner?*

The story's about this nun who's assigned to take care of a rich single father's kids. Do nun factories really loan out their nuns for shit like this? Because if they do, I've got about three months worth of laundry that needs to be done. At any rate, the dame they send over isn't very good at nunning (and all that really requires is a little praying, a little fasting, and maybe some light lezzing out), and if you ask me she's not so hot with kids either: within days they're all wearing clothes made out of old curtains and running around the countryside singing nonsense songs like a bunch of doped-up hippies. Trailer trash comes to Austria.

On the flip side, just like in every other movie or TV show that ever used this premise – *Who's the Boss*, *The Nanny*, *Mr. Belvedere* – the nun does manage to solve all of the kids' problems, although what those problems actually were is anybody's guess since none of the kids have any personalities. The only one who really stood out was the oldest daughter, and her only because she's pretty damn tasty. Give me half an hour with that one and the hills will be alive with the sound of her shrieking orgasm. It really makes me wonder what the hell is wrong with her little Nazi boyfriend. It's one thing to be a Nazi, but it's another thing to be so into being a Nazi that you stop liking pussy.

Of course the nun and the kids' dad eventually fall in love. Again, this is just like all the TV shows I mentioned previously. (Except *Mr. Belvedere*, although throwing in a twist like that might've have made that dumb, awful show worth watching.) The good times don't last for long, however, because shortly thereafter Dad decides to dodge the draft so the whole family has to flee the country. First though they put on this little show, and the dad intentionally sings a song during his part that he knows will completely irritate the Nazis. As you'll see, one sure-fire way to get movie critics to fawn all over your movie is to include a part where someone sings a song that completely irritates the Nazis. Me, I'd prefer it if this whole lot of caterwauling cretins just shut the fuck up.

Suggested Alternative: *The Quiet Earth* (1985)

#79

Rocky

(1976)

Punching

Fucking Rocky. How many goddamned movies can they make about a brain-damaged wop punching? It's even more retarded than Rocky himself will be by Part XII. Besides, any series that helped make the song "Eye of the Tiger" popular is bad by definition. Honestly, if there was ever an anthem for morons, "Eye of the Tiger" is it, and I have no qualms about putting that in writing because anyone who likes "Eye of the Tiger" enough to get pissed off about it either can't read, or doesn't have the time to kick my ass because he has to get to the gym. To tool for anus.

For those of you who don't know, Rocky is the story of a guy who's only good at two things: punching, and enunciating so that every word he says sounds like "duh." He spends the beginning of this movie trying to get with some emo chick, but then one day he gets a chance to punch the best puncher in the world, so with the help of the Penguin (who hates him at first, but is more than willing to ride his coattails once he gets famous), he starts to train for this once-in-a-lifetime opportunity to punch. He does have some doubts along the way and even tries to get out of it a couple of times (first by courting salmonella poisoning, and later by violating a bunch of FDA regulations on live TV in a blatantly transparent attempt to get arrested), but in the end he decides that he has to go the distance for the glory of love, so he steps up, gives it his all, and loses anyway. Ha ha! What an asshole. Oh, and spoiler warning.

So far there's been like ten sequels to this movie – the most notable being Part III where he fights Mr. T, and Part IV where he fights the Soviet Union and James Brown – and somehow each one managed to be stupider than all of the others put together. In short, if you only see one Rocky movie in your entire life, don't.

Bonus drinking game: Drink every time Rocky says "yo" or "y'know."

Medical disclaimer: If you actually do this, you will die.

Suggested Alternative: *Penitentiary III* (1987)

#78

Louisiana Story

(1948)
Drama

Do you know why tree-huggers invented the word *wetlands?* Because nobody wants to save a goddamned *swamp*. Swamps are full of leeches and crocodiles and yellow malaria, and the less of them we have around the better. Sure, if we drained all the swamps we might kill off some rare frog or something, but who cares? Honestly, when's the last time you needed a rare frog for anything? That's what I thought.

Speaking of frogs, this flick takes place in Cajun country. (You like how I did that?) When they show us a bunch of nature and then an oil rig going up I knew exactly where this was headed: break out your *Mark Trail* coloring book, because it's time to whine about the environment! For those of you who don't recognize the reference, *Mark Trail* is that comic strip with all the animal trivia ("Fun Fact: Beavers eat half their weight in gold every day!"). You know, the one you always skim over? *Mark Trail* is almost always about saving the environment. Hey, I just now realized that the name "Mark Trail" is a pun. Those fucking assholes.

Now, I fully expected a real story to kick in sooner or later here, most likely beginning when the oil guys set off the local environmental midgets by accidentally blowing up the ocean or wiping out an endangered species of tick or something. But the joke was on me this time, because as it turns out *this movie has no fucking story*. It's just this little retarded kid named Napoleon Guadalupe Anastasia Horsemeat Rodriguez (or something like that) wandering around the bayou (that's French for "wetlands"), killing animals for no good reason. (It's okay for *him* to kill them, because he doesn't vote Republican.) Oh, and every once in a while the oil rig guys, ignoring every OSHA regulation in the book, let him come on board and watch them work. Eventually he's just strolling in and out of the place, barefoot, whenever he pleases, including during emergency situations. I think he was even peaking on acid once.

AND THAT'S ALL THAT HAPPENS! Even introducing a gun in the last few minutes (and giving it to the retarded kid) doesn't result in any action. At one point I *think* the tard's pet raccoon got eaten by an alligator, but this whole sequence was so incomprehensible that I'm still not sure. First the raccoon's in the water, then it's bone dry, then it's in the water again, then it's a completely different raccoon, then it's on the Space Shuttle... Nice editing, idiots. Speaking of the raccoon, they waste entirely too much time on its goddamned antics. I found this especially annoying because I hate raccoons - they're evil creatures, in league with the Devil. You know what's a fun trick? Raccoons like to wash their food before they eat it, so if you ever encounter one, give it a sugar cube. See, the OCD little bastard will almost always try to rinse it off in the nearest stream or his water dish or something, and when he does, it'll disintegrate on him! Ha ha! Fuck you, raccoon.

Suggested Alternative: *Netherworld* (1992)

🎞️🎞️🎞️🎞️🎞️

#77

🎞️🎞️🎞️🎞️🎞️

Apocalypse Now
(1979)
War

Why are Vietnam vets such pussies? You never hear a dude who fought in World War Part 2 whine for decades at a time about it, tears streaming down his face, and then ask you for money because his kid is really sick, see, and he needs five more dollars for medicine. And hell, Nazis are a lot more hardcore than some chump named "Charlie." Seriously, what sounds scarier? "Here come the Nazis!" or "Here comes Charlie! You know, from payroll." It's a no-brainer.

The main Vietnam vet in this movie is no exception to the rule (one of the first things he does is get drunk and cry), but fortunately for us he generally gets pushed into the background while badasses like the cat who likes the smell of napalm in the morning take center stage. In fact, there's so much awesome, crazy shit going on that sometimes the main guy's whining is drowned out altogether, which is probably why this Vietnam flick makes so many 100 Best lists and hippie shit like *Born on the Fourth of July* (1989) doesn't. Some of the better bits include a helicopter attack scene that actually makes classical music seem cool (suck it, *Fantasia*), and the part where completely insane shit is popping off everywhere and this one soldier, all casual like, suddenly mentions that he's on acid. I love it when people drop acid in utterly inappropriate situations. Which is why I'm legally barred from working with children or operating industrial machinery in the state of Iowa.

The thing this movie is most famous for though is having the lamest ending in history. Honestly, the whole fucking movie builds this Kurtz clown up and builds him up and builds him up and when we finally meet him all he does is ramble incoherently for a while and then fall over. Welcome to me on most weekends. For real, it was more of a shocker when Silent Bob suddenly talked at the end of *Clerks*. What a fucking ripoff. When people say the journey is the reward, this movie is exactly what they're talking about. Well, either that or they're just talking crap, because let's face it, only complete tools say annoying, trite shit like "The journey is the reward."

Note: The guy who made this movie went back and George Lucased it at some point, but all he added was a bunch of French people complaining. I'd avoid that version.

Suggested Alternative: *More American Graffiti* (1979)

#76

Unforgiven

(1992)
Western

Most old-time westerns were about rustlin' cattle or people having a big gunfight at the Asshole Corral, but it seems like most westerns these days are about the end of the wild, wild west. Here's an idea: if you're so excited that it ended, stop making movies about it.

This one starts with some guy cutting up a whore, which is a pretty good way to kick off a movie. Seriously, think how much better *The Sound of Music* would be if it started out like that. The United Association of Whores (the whore union) is pretty pissed off about this, so they take up a collection and hire this amateur gunslinger to whack the guys responsible. The gunslinger decides he needs a little help though, so he tracks down Dirty Harry himself and asks him to lend a hand. At first Dirty Harry refuses because ever since he got married he's been completely pussywhipped and his vagina has swelled to almost epic proportions, but then he remembers that his wife is dead so he abandons his kids to be eaten by Indians and off they go.

Things do get a mite complicated when the two main guys find out that the law in those there parts is treating the whore-cutter like a star quarterback who raped a coed the weekend before the biggest "the big game" of the year, but you know that's not gonna stop Dirty fucking Harry so before (too) long the bad guys all get what's coming to them, including one dude who's blown away while he's on the shitter. This is the same way Vinnie Barbarino's character eats it in *Pulp Fiction* (Best Movie Ever Made #72). Apparently, not unlike having one of your characters sing a song that irritates the Nazis, having one of them shoot somebody who's pinching off a loaf is a real critic-pleaser.

Fun Fact: "Unforgiven" isn't a word.

Suggested Alternative: *The Gambler Returns: The Luck of the Draw* (1991)

#75

All Quiet on the Western Front

(1930)

War

One thing I like about 18-year-olds is that they're always willing to go off to war while I stay home drinking Mai Tais and fucking their girlfriends, and this movie begins with some kraut professor convincing a bunch of stupid kids to do just that. I thought professors were all supposed to be super liberal? Maybe that's just in the States.

The kids are pretty pumped at first, because they have no idea that war mostly entails being yelled at by a guy too dumb to get promoted beyond sergeant, fighting rats for food, and dying in horror. Well, their loss is our gain: we see people blown up, blinded, mowed down with machine guns, stabbed with bayonets, bludgeoned, rifle-whipped... In the best part, a dude gets exploded and there's nothing left but his hands! There's also this running gag about a pair of really nice boots that gets passed around. Whenever the joker wearing them bites the bucket, someone else takes them. I wonder if they'd do the same thing if they found out one of the guys had an especially comfy pair of underwear? People usually shit themselves when they die, so probably not.

I don't want to play down the bad things that happen though. For example, in one part a few of the guys are so hard up that they actually fuck some fat chicks. War really is hell.

Eventually two of the guys take some shrapnel, and things finally start looking up for them. First off, they end up in the hospital next to this crazy bastard named "Hamacher" who gets the best line in the entire movie:

HAMACHER: "I got a crack in the head and they gave me a certificate stating that 'Josef Hamacher is periodically not responsible for his actions.' And ever since then, Hamacher has been having a grand time!"

Plus, getting hurt in a war is like winning the world's crappiest lottery, because if you're busted up bad enough you usually get to go home. Of course, some nuns might have to saw your leg off first, but hey, that's the price you pay for freedom.

Suggested Alternative: Claim you're gay, have flat feet, and hate all other races. Bonus: this can also get you out of jury duty.

#74

Tokyo Story

(1953)
Drama

Philadelphia Story, Louisiana Story, Tokyo Story... It'd be nice if some of the 100 Best Movies Ever Made could show a little imagination once in a while. This one is about some wheezin' Japanese geezers who go to Tokyo to visit their family. If this was an Archie comic book they would've condensed the whole thing down to two panels and called it "Nip Trip," but this movie is *two hours and fifteen minutes long,* and if you want to know how long two hours and fifteen minutes can really be, check out one of the first conversations the grandparents have:

GRANDMOTHER: "Do you have the air cushion?"
GRANDFATHER: "Didn't I give it to you?"
GRANDMOTHER: "It's not here."
GRANDFATHER: "I'm sure I gave it to you."
GRANDMOTHER: "Really?"
GRANDMOTHER: "I still can't find it."
GRANDFATHER: "No? It must be there."
GRANDFATHER: "Oh, here it is."

GRANDMOTHER: "You found it?"
GRANDFATHER: "Yes, I did."

Jesus fucking Christ, kill me now. These two did surprise me a couple of times – like when they complain that their kids don't live in a "livelier" part of the city (apparently they were hoping to score some blow, kick it at the clubs, and maybe cap a honky or two), or when the old man gets utterly tanked and the cops have to bring him home – but for the most part it's all just as boring and annoying as when *your* senile Japanese relatives come for a visit. Needless to say their family does their best to get rid of them by pawning them off on every relation imaginable and even booking them into a hotel at one point. Finally the old fogies take the hint and go home, where the grandma immediately gets sick and dies, I assume just to spite everyone. The best thing about this part is the doctor's diagnosis:

DOCTOR: "It's not a good sign that's she's still in a coma."

I guess that's why he has the medical degree and I don't. For the record, other bad signs would include being on fire, or if her entire head was missing. At any rate, it's safe to say that this tragedy has taught everyone a valuable, if unbelievably boring, lesson, probably about family or something. Amazingly enough though, the damn movie still isn't over! It rambles on for another *half a fucking hour!* Christ. I never wanted Gamera to show up more in my entire life.

Suggested Alternative: *Terror of Mechagodzilla* (1975)

#73

Seven Samurai

(1954)
Action

Here's something I don't understand. Old movies tend to be pretty corny, and I think most of us just let it slide because we assume that people simply didn't know any better back then. But every once in a while you'll catch an old movie like this one that feels like it was made just last week and isn't corny at all, so obviously at least a few people back in the day knew how to get the job done. Which means that the vast majority of old movies are even shittier than we previously believed. "Golden Age of Hollywood" my ass.

The plot is pretty basic: these whiny farmers keep getting it handed to them by some bandits, so they decide to round up seven samurai to kick the bandits' dicks in. If this sounds familiar, that's because they remade it as a western (*Seven Magnificent Bastards*) and at least two different sci-fi movies (*Star Wars* and *Battle Beyond the Network Stars*).

This original version is pretty good too, even without any cowboys or robots - when shit finally pops off there's tons of action and violence, and along the way there's quite a few bits that are legitimately funny. The best is when the main bad guy gets pissed off at two of his boys for trying to run away: "If anybody else turns yellow..." he says. Dude, you're Japanese - you're *all* yellow!

So this one's a pretty decent watch, but what would have made it ten times better is if they they could have worked in some ninjas. Everybody knows that ninjas are way cooler than samurai, mainly because they have tons of eerie powers. And no tits? Really? They could have solved both of these problems by replacing the samurai with ninjas, and then, after the bandits were defeated, the villagers could've rewarded the ninjas by turning over the seven hottest, nakedest girls in the village to be their wives. Seven Brides for Seven Ninjas. Now that sounds like a fucking movie.

Suggested Alternative: *Master of the Flying Guillotine* (1975)

#72

Pulp Fiction

(1994)
Action

Quentin Tarantino is an annoying, overrated hack who looks and talks like the guy you beat up in college for stalking your girlfriend. If my daughter brought home a guy who looked like Quentin Tarantino, I would kick the shit out of him before he got halfway through the door. And if she begged me to stop because it *really was* Quentin Tarantino, I'd kick the shit out of him again. Mainly for *Kill Bill: Vol. 1* (2003).

Don't get me wrong, his movies do have some funny speeches, but they all play out the exact same way and have the exact same ending: everyone congregates in one place, where they get into a huge shootout that's so violent, over the top, and out of control that you can't help being bored senseless. That's what makes *Pulp Fiction* so brilliant: the story jumps around in time, so they were able to spread the ending out through the entire movie which means that the damn thing actually has a chance to be about something.

Actually, there's a lot of shit in this flick that's genuinely awesome, like the glowing suitcase (sorry to ruin all your retard theories, but it's supposed to be full of Indiglo watches, bootleg Indiglo watches), the guy eating Fruit Brute, and the best response ever to some pretentious tool saying "I don't watch television." Besides "Oh, fuck you," of course. Plus it helped make heroin, cocaine, and shoving watches up your ass hip again, which boosted the value of all three of my side businesses considerably.

Pulp Fiction isn't perfect of course. The biggest mistake is when it opens with the dictionary definition for "pulp." It's always a bush league move to start with the definition of the thing you're going to write about. Think about it - if you're assigned to write about something and the first thing you have to do is look it up in the goddamned dictionary to see what it even is, it's a pretty safe bet that you're not exactly an expert on the subject. When you see a magazine or newspaper article do this, you're almost certainly dealing with a pinhead who doesn't know what the hell he's talking about. Other problems with this flick include the supafine brunette not showing us her tits, the part where the black guy takes it up the ass – which I assure you no one wanted to see – and the fact that it made Vinnie Barbarino popular again. Also, is there anyone on Earth who didn't want to see Bruce Willis's frog girlfriend die a slow, horrible death? Every time that bitch opened her mouth I wanted to punch her in the fucking face. A battered woman's shelter would turn her away, on the grounds that she probably deserved it.

And, finally, five dollars isn't all that much for a pretty fuckin' good milkshake anymore. Hell, the ones from McDonald's are three dollars, and they taste like packing foam. Ol' Quentin really should've anticipated that and made it a twenty-dollar milkshake. Especially since they make such a big deal out of it.

Suggested Alternative: *Avenging Disco Godfather* (1979)

#71

The Grapes of Wrath

(1940)
Road Trip

I'll bet you know this one; they made you read it in high school[5], so naturally you watched the movie instead. Except the movie leaves out the bit about the turtle, so you probably still got an F. In the end the book is all about the turtle. Ask anyone.

Okay, so the movie version starts out with... Hey, "Technical Director: Tom Collins." That sounds like a pretty good idea, hang on a minute. Oh, and if you'd like to join me:

TOM COLLINS
2 oz. gin
2 oz. lemon juice
1 teaspoon simple syrup
Top off with soda water
Garnish with a lemon and a cherry

---

5 Unless you took dummy English, in which case I believe you read *Twilight*.

Ahhh, that really hits the spot. Some folks will try to tell you that this drink is only for old people, but don't you believe them. Okay, where were we? Oh yeah, *The Grapes of Wrath*. The movie starts by explaining how there's never enough rain in the Dust Bowl, so all the farms there went belly-up. If the Dust Bowl doesn't get much rain, why would anyone try to grow a farm there in the first place, you ask? Because everyone in this flick is a wacky, zany character, that's why! You'll see what I mean right away: the story opens with the main guy hitching a ride, and when the driver starts asking him all these nosy questions the main guy tells him that he just got out of the pen - for murder! Ha ha! The look on the driver's face is priceless. This bit effectively sets the scene for the madcap antics to follow.

When the main guy gets home he finds out that his family had to pull up stakes because the company that owns all the farms in the area decided to foreclose. The part where they dot the i by running over this one farmer's house with a bulldozer is priceless. Ha ha! Loser. Needless to say the farmers are less than pleased, but there's no samurai for hire in the Dust Bowl and they're not even sure who to blame anyway. "Who do we shoot?" asks one cat. Ha ha!

They're completely out of options at this point, so they pile all their shit onto their beat-up trucks (Just like the Beverly Hillbillies! Ha ha!) and set out for California, because supposedly there's jobs there. The main guy's grandpa doesn't want to leave though, so they have to drug him! (Just like Mr. T on *The A-Team*! Ha ha!) Of course these hicks opt to get their kicks on Route 66, and naturally they get into all these comical scrapes along the way: they run out of gas (Ha ha!), they get a flat tire (Ha ha!), and they even have a chase with the cops. Oh, and along the way grandpa and grandma *both* die! It's just like *National Lampoon's Vacation* (1983), except twice as funny! And here's the corker - when they finally get to California – are you ready for this? – Walley World is closed, by which I mean there's no jobs after all! Ah ha ha ha ha ha ha ha ha ha ha ha!!!

Man, what a terrific movie. I laughed and laughed.

Suggested Alternative: *The Grapes of Death* (1978)

#70

Goodfellas

(1990)
Drama

Note: This is a review of a mob movie, so I'm going to use the word "fuck" as many times as possible.

Every time I see this movie I think the same thing:

Shut the fuck up, you little piece of shit.

Yeah, you know who I'm talking about. Fuck that guy. Fuck his big fucking mouth, fuck the fact that he's only four feet tall, fuck his psychotic outbursts over inconsequential shit, and, while we're at it, fuck his mother in the mouth. Seriously, you meet assholes like this all the time in real life and they suck beyond belief, yet for some reason everybody finds his bullshit in this movie all hilarious. Well it's not, it's fucking annoying, which is why my favorite part of this flick is when that little assfuck gets beaten senseless in a field and then buried alive, even though that actually happens in *Casino* (1995). Seriously, he can suck my dick.

The only person in this flick who's more obnoxious is the main guy's moronic fucking girlfriend-cum-wife. "What, he's in the mob? That's unpossible!" You brainless twat. Maybe if that twenty-pound helmet you call your hair hadn't caved your goddamned skull in you'd be able to put two and two together and come up with something besides "He's so dreamy because has a nice car!"

As you can see, the characters in this movie are annoying, but that's okay because it has plenty of violence and at least some of it is directed at the two individuals I previously mentioned. On the other hand – big surprise here – there is a serious lack of tits. For real, why don't mob movies have more tits in them? Mob guys like pussy, and they generally have a lot of it hanging around, so what the fuck? I especially wouldn't have minded seeing what the main guy's cokehead girlfriend was sporting - she is fucking *primo*. And is that a young Illeana Douglas creeping around? Uh, *yum*. Seriously, I dig me some 'Leana.

You know, now that I think about it, a general lack of rack isn't the only weird thing about mob movies. For instance, have you ever noticed that they're the only type of movie that's allowed to get away with not having a plot? Think about any mob movie you've ever seen: 90% of the time it's just one random bit after another, until everyone finally dies or gets busted, the end. If a horror flick or a comedy tries to get away with that the critics are all over their shit, but when a mob flick does it, fuck it, it's one of the best movies ever made. I think movie critics are more afraid to cross mob movies than they would be to cross the actual mob. Honestly, movie critics, you need to man (or vag) up; not every mob movie is the greatest thing since sliced butter. Have you not seen *Mobsters* (1991)?

Actually they probably haven't, because nobody did.

Suggested Alternative: *Casino* (1995), obviously.

#69

The General

(1926)
Comedy

This flick is so old that it doesn't have sound, despite the fact that we had recorded sound long before it came out, which is why I've always found the whole concept of "silent movies" to be at least as suspect as the O.J. Simpson Mars landing. And did you ever wonder what the people in silent movies were *really* saying? I mean, you'll see some cat babbling on and on for like five minutes and then the title card will tell you that he said "What?" or "Let's go!" or something. What about all that stuff we missed? Was everything he said actually applicable to the situation, or was he just ad-libbing whatever popped into his head? Hell, for all we know these people are totally talking trash! "Hey, everyone watching this, go fuck your mother!" You know what would be an awesome project? Watching all these old movies with a professional lip reader so we can finally find out what the hell is really going on. And, more importantly, whether or not any of these actors need to have their lights punched out. Seriously, who wants in on this? AFI? IFC? *Sight & Sound*? I'm just waiting for the funding.

The story is about this Johnny Reb Civil War cat who chases down some Yankee spies who stole a Rebel train. Later though the shoe's on the other table when he ends up spying on *them* and stealing one of *their* trains. None of this really matters though, because it's all just an excuse for the main guy to do a bunch of insane stunts. I'll have to admit, some of them are pretty impressive too, and at least they're realistic - there's no flying eighty feet into the air and then safely landing on top of a barn, or two cars pulling up just in time to save Die Hard from being hit by a third car that's spiraling through the air, or any similar cretinous shit. I'm not sure why this is considered a comedy though; the stuff the main cat does is amazing and clever, but I really wouldn't call much of it *funny*. Maybe the humorosity comes from the fact that the main guy is going through this huge ordeal primarily to rescue a chick who, quite frankly, has a pretty fat ass. Sure, standards of beauty were different back then, but really, no they weren't.

Still, even if there aren't that many laughs this flick does end with an honest-to-god train falling through a goddamned bridge into a fucking river. Even a hundred years later this bit is still pretty fucking awesome; you just don't see that kind of wasteful, over-the-top destruction in movies anymore. Nowadays, they'd just send some P.A. to film the cliff on everyone else's day off and then use a laptop to add a cartoon train later. It's so fucking weak. And the train crash leads to the one part of the movie that actually *is* funny: the look on the face of the clown who ordered the train to cross the bridge in the first place, even though the bridge was obviously on fire. They're probably still garnishing his great-great-great-great-

great-grandkids' wages for that boner.

Incidentally, despite the way this flick ends, I'm pretty sure the South lost the Civil War.

Suggested Alternative: *Buck Privates* (1941)

#68

The Apartment

(1960)
Comedy

The main guy in this flick lets his superiors use his apartment to cheat on their wives so he can get ahead at the office. Ha ha! He's a complete scumbag! His sleazy scheme goes awry though when he falls for legendary spank magnet Shirley MacLaine, who he's apparently been stalking for some time:

SHIRLEY MACLAINE: "How do you know where I live?"
MAIN GUY: "I even know who you live with. Sister, brother-in-law... I know when you were born, and where. I know all sorts of things about you."

What a creep. The real problem though is that Shirley just happens to be the very girl his boss has been screwing at his place. Eventually the boss screws her in more ways than one, so she has one of those drama-queen chick-style breakdowns and tries to commit suicide - right there in the main guy's pad! Ha ha! It's a farce! Then she flips out when she can't score any rock and throws several bottles of wine out the window at a passing police car. Oh, wait, that was the last girl I had over to *my* apartment. What Shirley MacLaine does is even funnier - she dies! Ha! I'm kidding, but seriously, I wouldn't put it past this movie. What really happens is that the main guy finds her when he comes home – with someone else's wife in tow, I might add – and they manage to pump all the pills and semen out of her stomach just in time.

Wow. I've purchased snuff films from child molesters who weren't as degenerate as the people in this movie. And I haven't even gotten to the sexual harassment, the rumor-mongering, or the hilarious illegal abortion-oriented misunderstanding which leads to a savage beating.

Obviously this should be an awesome movie, especially seeing as Shirley MacLaine just happened to be the hottest piece of tail who existed on Earth in 1960. Unfortunately, for all intents and purposes it was still the 1950's (due to a clerical error, the 1960's didn't actually begin until 1965), so there's not a single scene where she gets naked. To make matters worse, this is supposed to be a comedy but it isn't the least bit funny. Imagine *Three's Company* played kinda straight and you'll get the general idea. This movie has aged better than Shirley MacLaine did, though. By the 1980's she was so used-up and crazy that she was writing books about discovering Atlantis via ESP and shit. One more example why you should never marry someone solely for their looks. At the very least they should have money, too.

Suggested Alternative: Running this hustle for real

#67

Sunset Blvd.

(1950)
Drama

This writer gets a flat tire and ends up crashing at some run-down mansion inhabited by a crazy old lady and her weird-ass butler. Then, late that night, he looks out the window and sees these two nut-jobs burying a monkey in the backyard. How this doesn't turn out to be a horror movie is beyond me. Instead, it's mainly about the old lady, an out-to-pasture actress (i.e. over 30) who wants to make a comeback. "Don't call it a comeback!" she says. Well, she could have.

This writer knows a good thing when he sees it, so, undeterred by the monkey business (heh), he decides to stick around and freeload off the crazy old bat for a while. Now that's one thing, but eventually the sick fuck actually starts tapping her fossilized pussy! Dude, she's *over 30*. After a while he gets tired of choking on a cloud of dust every time he hits it so he decides to be on his way, but he just can't resist pushing the crazy old lady's buttons first, despite the fact that she's waving a gun around at this point. If you've even seen *Snapped!* on the Oxygen Channel you can probably guess what happens next.

So is any of this entertaining? Well, watching a ridiculous has-been make a fool of herself is always good for a laugh or two (Paula Abdul), but what's truly hysterical is how the main actress in this movie plays the old lady. She's not quite hag-like enough to actually play a hag, so she tries to make herself look the part by sucking back her lips so that her teeth are always exposed and constantly bugging her eyes out like a chameleon that took too much speed. Jack Nicholson as the Joker was more subtle.

And I have to ask, what is with the ending? Some crazy broad is taking pot-shots at him, but instead of running like hell the main guy just keeps strolling along like it's no big thing. Okay, maybe he thought she ate that first bullet herself, but I would've hit the dirt just in case. I mean really, dude, you just spent the better part of a year boffing a dame old enough to be your mother just because she bought you a few clothes and a cigarette case. There's no point in playing it cool now.

Suggested Alternative: *Riot on Sunset Strip* (1967)

#66

Snow White and the Seven Dwarfs

(1937)
Musical

This? *This* is the greatest cartoon ever made? Bull. Shit. I suppose I'm willing to concede that the greatest cartoon ever made is by Disney because they steal only the best, but how is this better than *Aladdin* (1992) or *Toy Story 2* (1999) or hell, even *Sleeping Beauty* (1959), with that huge, kick-ass dragon at the end? Is it because it was the first? First isn't always best, assholes; if it was, you'd be married to that chick with the asthma who let you fuck her on your 16th birthday. Or maybe the critics decided this cartoon is important because Disney has been recycling shit from it ever since. Ever see *Disney's Copyrighted Adventures of the Gummi Bears*? Zummi Gummi is just a re-hashed Doc, except furry and sans pants. Now that I think about it, Disney does seems endlessly convinced that the Seven Dwarfs are all iconic and shit, even though kids are terrified of them and nobody can actually name more than three. Get your heads out of the sand, Disney.

Okay, everyone knows the story. One of those comedy/tragedy masks lives in this witch's mirror and feeds her completely out-of-control ego by constantly telling her that she's the hottest piece of ass on the planet. But then, one day, the mirror tells her that this trick Snow White just took the title, so the witch decides to take the upstart out. If you ask me, the witch's plan to bump off Snow White is way too complicated, not to mention completely unnecessary. Honestly, just cut the bitch. She won't be so beautiful then, with a big old scar down her face.[6] Of course the witch's scheme fails, but Snow White ends up lost in the woods, where the kindly forest critters take pity on her. Why do the forest critters like Snow White so much? They never say, but I heard that sometimes animals are attracted to women who are menstruating, so we'll assume that's it.

Whatever the reason, the animals lead her to the home of the Seven Dwarfs, a bunch of short guys with big noses who hoard diamonds. In other words, they're Jews. She shacks up with the Jews and everything's hunky-dory for a while, until the witch gets wind of the fact that she isn't croaked and shows up with a poisoned apple. Snow Not-So-Bright eats the apple and dies, the end.

Oh, wait, I almost left out the most twisted part. The Seven Jews hold a little funeral for Snow White, and this prince who happens along decides to crash it. The prince, overcome by her

---

6   If you ask me, the wicked queen should just chill the fuck out, because I think she's a lot hotter than Snow White anyway. Plus she's wicked, which is a definite bonus in bed.

beauty even in death, kisses Snow White and the magic of his love makes her pop back to life. It all sounds so sweet and romantic, until you think about this: if Prince Necrophilia had stumbled onto Snow White's corpse after the dwarfs had left, what do you think he would have done with it then?

Suggested Alternative: *Song of the South* (1946)

```
□□□□□□□
```
#65
```
□□□□□□□
```

An American in Paris

(1951)
Musical

AKA *Hell Comes to Frogtown*. Ah ha ha ha ha ha ha! Brilliant.

It's a question that has haunted mankind for centuries: why do musicals suck? Music doesn't suck, and movies don't suck – unless you're talking like *The Mummy Returns* (2001) or something – so why does combining them almost always result in something that makes you want to saw your own ears off? I think it's because most people can't concentrate on two things at the same time. Have you ever seen someone texting while they're driving? And then they crash into something? That's exactly what I'm talking about. It's way too hard to come up with good songs *and* a good story, so one of them is always compromised, which ultimately brings down the whole damn hullabaloo.

Take this musical, for example. It's about some guys roaming around Paris, slacking ass and being low-key pimps, which should be at least passably entertaining. But the story is what you'd call "slight;" it's mainly just an excuse for the main guy to dance, and for his buddies to sing and play music. In other words, it's the 1951 version of *Breakin'* (1984), except after the last show of the night everyone's car wasn't broken into.

The plot grinds into low gear when the main guy starts making time with this teen-aged piece who, unbeknownst to him, is engaged to his friend-in-law. This complicates things not only for the friend-in-law, but also for the connecting friend *and* the old bag who's been fronting the main guy money in the hopes that *she* can get into his pants. (Actually she's not that old, and she's hardly a bag, but she's not nineteen either so sorry baby, but you lose.) Not that Teen-Aged Tessie discourages any of this, because, frankly, she's a whore. She is droolingly hot though, even if she does have a mouth you could fit an entire bowling ball into. Fortunately you really only notice this when she smiles, so if she was my girl I'd just make sure she was angry all the time, which really isn't that difficult. Just being my girl will usually get you there.

To be fair the song & dance bits are nearly tolerable until the very last one, which is just too damn much - it's like 15 minutes long, real time! Thank God the main chick participates in it - if it wasn't for her legs there'd be almost no way to stand it. The worst thing about it though is that unlike the other songs, which at least fit into the story, it doesn't make any goddamned sense. Seriously, if the super high-caliber chick you were after left the party with another guy, would you conjure up some huge, intricate fantasy about doing a dance number with her? Or would you dream up a more intimate, personal fantasy, like say one where you pleasured her with a cucumber while she hung upside-down and took your whole package, sack and all, into her humongous Mr. Sardonicus mouth? If this movie had ended with fifteen minutes of *that,* they might've been onto something.

It's all completely moot anyway, since the other guy, who's been clued in by this point, brings her back two seconds later and relinquishes all claims. I guess he didn't want her anymore once he realized he'd been parking it in a two-cock garage.

Suggested Alternative: *An American Werewolf in Paris* (1997)

#64

Ugetsu Monogatari

(1953)
Horror

I'm not surprised that we're over a third of our way through this list and this is the first horror movie we've seen. Movie critics hate horror movies, and even when they're forced to pick one and admit that it's good they generally choose something like this that's in black & white *and* has subtitles. Movie critics are so fucking pretentious.

Now, I have to start off here by admitting that I really don't understand one of the two main guys in this flick. He wants to go to the big city, and when he finds out that this other cat is going there he offers to pull the guy's big, heavy cart if he can come with. Here's an idea: why not walk there yourself, and *not* pull a big, heavy cart? If you don't know the way, just follow the other guy! What a complete fucking moron.

Obviously his goal in the big city should be purchasing a brain, but what he really wants is to become a samurai. Samurai used to be big heroes in Japan and every kid wanted to be one, like how today's kids all want to be inner-city drug dealers. The samurai won't take him because he can't afford any official samurai gear though, so he officially throws in with the cart guy so as to earn the necessary bread. See, there's a war on, so the guy with the cart is making a killing selling homemade dishes and pottery. Yeah, I don't get it either. Maybe both armies ran out of arrows and are reduced to throwing crockery at each other. There's some more putzing around regarding all of this, but eventually these two clowns split up and have completely unrelated adventures. Because *that's* dramatically satisfying.

In the first adventure, this creepy chick invites the guy who owns the cart to her pad because she claims she wants to buy some of his crap. As it turns out though, she's really just hot to trot. I *knew* there was no way "I wanted to taste sake from your cups," meant anything other than "Fuck me hard, studly-san." Now, cart guy is already married, but he starts boning this creepy bitch for the long haul anyway, until one day when a priest with a goofy hat clues him in that she's really a ghost! So he extracts himself from that situation only to come home and find out that his wife is a ghost too! The other ghost was way better looking though, so I'd say he definitely blew it.

The second guy, meanwhile, finally manages to become a samurai by claiming to have cut off some dude's head, even though he really found the head laying on the ground. ("Anybody lose this? Last chance.") Pretty soon he's super-famous, but then *his* wife turns up, endlessly whining and bitching because he abandoned her in the process and she got gang-raped and had to become a hooker. Oh, boo hoo.

Eventually he abandons his dream of being a samurai just to get her to shut the hell up, but even though he's done exactly what she wants she still keeps nagging and riding him about it. Fucking rag - he should've cut *her* goddamned head off.

Suggested Alternative: *Kung Fu Zombie* (1982)

#63

A Clockwork Orange

(1971)

Science Fiction

In my experience, most people who claim to like this flick just watch the beginning over and over again and then turn it off when the main guy finally gets busted. I kind of get it though, because it's fun to watch main guy and his gang run amok, but as a whole this movie is pretty tiresome. Sure, it's got assault, rape, brainwashing – all the shit people like – but it's kind of hard to take any of it seriously when it centers on a bunch of supposed thugs who dress like endless queers. And what is with the fucking slang? Half of it sounds like baby talk: "eggiwegs" for "eggs," "stakie-wakes" for "steak." I'm supposed to be intimidated by these guys? Aw, does the liddle dwoogs need some milky-milk? Fucking pussies. Besides, anyone who makes up their own slang is a total Jarvis.

Stanley "The Brick" Kubrick, the guy who made this movie, sure didn't have a very good idea what the future would be like either. Everyone still has a typewriter? Even movies made in the 1950's knew that we'd be using computers by now. I also wasn't too happy when I paused the DVD and read the top ten list in the record store: the Sparks are going to make a comeback? I sure hope he's wrong about that one; if I ever hear "Angst in My Pants" again it'll be too goddamned soon.

Not that I'm implying anything here, but speaking of the Sparks, there are too many penises in this movie, too. We've got people being hit in the penis, someone beaten to death with a ceramic penis, graffiti of penises, even actual penises. Nobody wants to see that shit, Kubrick. No, not even gay dudes. Looking back, there's really only one thing I like about this movie: the Minister of the Interior is played by the old guy from *The Young Ones* (1982-1984) who asked people to refrain from molesting his parrot. That bit always cracks me up

Frankly, if running amok is what you're into and you're not motivated enough to do it yourself, there are way better movies about it that you could be watching. ⬇

Suggested Alternatives: *Romper Stomper* (1992), *The Boys Next Door* (1985)

#62

A Streetcar Named Desire

(1951)

Drama

"A Pumpernickel Named Fuck Me!" For real, I don't care how you justify it, "A Streetcar Named Desire" is a stupid, fruity name for a movie. (For a play, not so much, because plays are fruity by definition.) And I understand that the cat who wrote this was, in fact, gay? I'd expect it if his name was like "Florida Jones" or "Unincorporated Clearwater Smith", but *Tennessee Williams?* That's way too macho of a name to squander on a homo. He should've had that changed right away, and then sold the "Tennessee Williams" trademark to the cat who wrote "The Old Man and the Sea". True story: that "Old Man and the Sea" cat was so hardcore that he once shot himself in both legs while trying to kill a shark with a Tommy gun. Plus he was drunk at the time, probably.

Story: this chick invites her ugly, obnoxious, drama queen of a sister to stay with her, and it takes the dripping whore less then five seconds flat to start throwing her pussy at her brother-in-law like it was attached to a bungee cord. She also macks on one of his friends, hits on the goddamned *paperboy,* and, frankly, I'm pretty sure there was a part where she was gonna dyke out with her own sister if they hadn't been interrupted. This flick was obviously based on a play because all they do is talk and nobody ever goes anyplace, although like most flicks based on plays they do slip in a couple unnecessary scenes that go down in other locations, like a bowling alley, just to remind us that we're actually watching a movie. Truth be told, that moment of sudden clarity when I realize that I'm watching the movie version of play never fails to piss me off. If I wanted to see a play, I'd go to a goddamned play, you underhanded assholes.

I will say though, as much as this sucks I did like the way the main cat handled his business. He says a lot of awesome shit, but the best is when he gives his sister-in-law a bus ticket back home for her birthday. Ha ha! If you've got some freeloading relative squatting at your place, you could learn a lot from this guy.

Suggested Alternative: *Madhouse* (1990)

████████

#61

████████

The Silence of the Lambs

(1991)

Horror

If there's one movie I'm tired of hearing clueless pinheads blather endlessly on about, it's motherfucking *Silence of the* motherfucking *Lambs*. "Dude, you haven't seen *Silence of the Lambs*???" I've haven't taken it up the ass either, what's it to you? Well, now I've finally seen it and I can't say I'm very impressed. It's mainly just a series of fake-outs (like the part where we think the FBI is about to raid the killer's house, but then it turns out they're raiding the wrong place and someone else is actually at the killer's door), with some gay cross-dressing and lots of talking thrown in. I'm so impressed.

This movie didn't actually invent the super-genius serial killer who won't shut the fuck up, but it definitely made him popular enough to become annoying. But even though everyone mostly remembers Hannibal "the Chatty Cannibal" Lecter, the killer the FBI is primary concerned with in this flick is some gay, cross-dressing fag named "Buffalo Bill," whose goal is to make a Disney-style Dalmatian puppy coat, except out of fat chicks. Naturally no one's mourning the loss of a few fat chicks, that is until Buffalo Bill kidnaps this senator's daughter, at which point everyone goes into DEFCON 4 because as we all know senator's daughters, like cops, are way more important than the rest of us. Don't you love how movies expect us to get especially pumped up when someone says "He's a cop killer"? Never mind that the bad guy in question has already murdered like twenty people who weren't cops.

This movie isn't a total wash though. The main chick looks the hottest she ever has, and considering her age now, probably ever will, and Hannibal the Banana Bowl does slaughter a few hapless idiots in fairly gory ways, plus puts some moderately clever shit over on everyone besides. Although the part where he wears a dead guy's face to escape – another fake-out – was so obvious that I saw it coming a mile and a half away, at night, with sunglasses on.

Not a lot of people realize this, but this movie is actually the sequel to a 1980's flick called *Manhunter* (1986). There was also a *Buffalo Bill* TV series in the 1980's starring Dabney Coleman, but I'm not entirely sure how that ties in.

Suggested Alternative: *My Bloody Valentine* (1981 or 2009)

#60

Persona
(1966)
Drama

The MGM version of this DVD essentially tells you the big twist right on the back of the case. I'll bet there's a guy in charge of sales over at MGM who looks at some chart every day and wonders why they don't sell more copies of *Persona*. Stupid assholes.

Not that anyone would want to buy this movie anyway. It starts by bombarding us with a bunch of random, pretentious crap. If it's so random, how do I know it's supposed to be pretentious, you may ask? Trust me, you can tell. Oh, and just for the homos, they also throw in some guy's dick. And what does all this have to do with the story? Nothing! Ha ha! Looks like you've fooled me again, 100 Best Movies Ever Made! Fuck you.

The actual story – what there is of it – begins when this nurse is assigned to take care of some actress who's being all flaky and self-absorbed and frankly just needs a good smack across her dick-massager. I think she's supposed to be in some sort of hospital, but her room is completely bare except for the bed she's laying on and one crappy wooden chair - there's no other furniture, no medical equipment, nothing. Thank you, ObamaCare.

Eventually the actress and the nurse both relocate to this beach house, where the nurse talks and talks and talks and talks, mostly about what a whore she is. I figured that with all this sex talk at the very least the two of them would eventually get it on. After all, the only real difference between porn and art is subtitles. They never do though, and the movie is more than half over before anything interesting happens, and even when it does it's not *that* interesting. Then, just to pad out the running time, the nurse gives a big speech explaining everything we just saw, and we have to listen to it *twice!* That's great for anyone who picked the wrong time to go to the bathroom, but for the rest of us it's totally redundant and unbelievably irritating. Although nowhere near as irritating as the fact that they didn't include any lesbo action.

Suggested Alternative: *Fight Club* (1999)

◨◨◨◨◨◨◨

#59

◨◨◨◨◨◨◨

The Birth of a Nation

(1915)
Drama

If you spend any time at all thinking about movies (beyond "Where can I download this movie for free?" I mean), you've probably wondered what the first movie ever made was. Well, the first movie ever was Thomas Edison's *Edison Kinetoscopic Record of a Sneeze* (1894), and it's just a few seconds of some guy sneezing.[7] Well, what did you expect? *RoboCop 2* (1990)? I know, I know, what you really mean is what was the first *real* movie ever made? Well, this is it, and naturally it's about the Ku Klux Klan saving the world! And even though we're so beyond politically correct these days that I can't even yell "Viva gordita!" outside the USCIS office without getting arrested, it's *still* considered one of the greatest movies of all time! *Ah ha ha ha ha ha ha!* If you ever needed definitive proof that movie critics are all just a bunch of mind-staggeringly out-of-touch white guys, this is it.

---

7   Actually, I have it on pretty good authority that the first movie Thomas Edison ever made was really called "My Neighbor's Tits," but we'll go with the official story.

And I definitely want to emphasize *guys,* because this movie is sexist too - at one point they're talking about war and they show us "The Woman's Part" which, they make pretty clear, is staying at home, crying. Girl Power! Needless to say this whole movie is in such staggeringly bad taste that it's endlessly fucking hilarious. For example, in the beginning this one chick shows up with a huge white kitty-cat - obviously they're trying to make it clear that she just arrived with her big, white pussy. What are the chances she'll get raped by a black guy before it's all over? Pretty high, I'd say. Other affronts to good taste and common sense include people drinking some concoction called "sweet potato coffee" and black people who talk like this: "Dem free-niggers f'um de N'of am sho' crazy. Fo' shizzle."

Plot-wise, the first half is your typical "war sucks" crap, but that's fine with me because we get to see plenty of the main honkies get wasted and good riddance because frankly they were a bunch of fops. Or, as we call them nowadays, "I'd sit back down if I were you, buddy." The true hilarity begins when the war is over: this cat who wants black people to be equal (of course he's the bad guy) puts out the word that they don't have to be slaves anymore. The desalinization process goes okay at first, but then some fool gives the former slaves free food *and* hats so they go on the rampage. Pretty soon they're voting and occasionally being found "not guilty" by juries. Unthinkable! Finally the main cracker just can't take it any more, so he invents the KKK, and not a moment too soon either because the main black guy has gone all Ming the Merciless and is trying to force this white chick to marry him, "While helpless whites look on." He almost gets away with it too, until the Klan comes riding in to give him and all his "homies" the what-for.[8]

For some reason it takes the Klan *forever* to get there though - I think a good ten minutes of this flick is just endless shots of the Klan riding to the rescue. Seriously, where are these assholes coming from? Canada? They do eventually arrive though and the day is saved. Hooray for the KKK! Fifty-ninth best movie ever made! White people have spoken!

Bonus: My copy of this DVD had a little trivia game on it, so I checked it out. One of the questions was "What is the alternate title of 'Birth of a Nation'?" and one of the answers you can pick is "K.K.K. O.K." Ha ha! It's good to see that some people haven't lost their sense of humor.

Suggested Alternative: *Brotherhood of Death* (1976)

---

8 Incidentally, I think it's cute how the Klansmen went and made little costumes for their horses too.

#58

L'Atalante

(1934)
Drama

The *L'Atalante* is a boat, and her captain just married some bimbo and moved her on board. Isn't it bad luck to bring a woman onto a ship? I guess he doesn't care if it is; in fact, he's so excited that as soon as they cast off he's trying to bone her right there on the deck. Before long the wife is truly hatin' it though. First off, the tub is a total dump. Even worse, the first mate is an animal hoarder and there are cats *everywhere:* they pop out entire litters of kittens right on the bed, they attack the captain's face, and, instead of a parrot (standard), the first mate actually has a cat riding around on his shoulder! I guess that makes him a pussy pirate. Ha! Seriously though, isn't it bad luck to bring cats onto a ship?

It gets even crazier - the first mate is a drunk too, not to mention a deranged pervert. He keeps his dead, gay lover's hands in a jar in his closet, and at one point he offers to show the captain's wife his "little man." His "little man" turns out to be a puppet, but this puppet is so fucking creepy that seeing the dude's dick probably would've been less disturbing. Worst of all though, he plays the accordion. The first mate does, I mean, not the puppet. Isn't it bad luck to bring an accordion onto a ship? It has to be - it's bad luck to bring an accordion anywhere. The girl doesn't seem to mind any of this though, and she spends so much time with the loon that her husband gets pissed off and karate chops her in the neck. *C'est l'amor!*

Eventually the newlyweds go ashore, where they meet this obnoxious dipshit who does card tricks and sells worthless hoohaws, knick-knacks, and paddy-whacks to the tourists. Plus he actually owns one of those "one man band" get-ups that I thought only existed in cartoons from the 1940's. This clown macks *all over* the main chick until her husband runs him off, but in some inexplicable manner this makes her realize that there's more to life than sailing around the world on a boat that reeks of cat piss with the constant threat of being kung fu'ed in the throat hanging over her head. So she runs away to Paris. When the captain finds out he's furious and sails off without her, but eventually he misses her, gets all depressed, and starts slacking off so much that the owner of the boat is on the verge of shit-canning everybody.

Knowing that there are few openings out there for "creepy, gay drunk with 80 cats" the first mate goes to Paris to find the wife so that she and the captain can reconcile, and naturally she just happens to be in one of the very first places he looks. How fucking convenient. Seriously, it takes me longer to find my car keys, and my place isn't even that big. Give me a fucking break.

Suggested Alternative: *Cabin Boy* (1994)

#57

Intolerance

(1916)
Drama

"Intolerance" hell, this flick should be called "Endurance." It's over three hours long! Do you realize how much I could have accomplished in the time I wasted watching this one movie? I could've gotten **so** drunk. And I like how it kicks off with a note explaining that the story is going to be about how bad hatred and intolerance are, never mind that the sucker who made it is the same cat who made *Birth of a Nation*, a movie entirely dedicated to hating the nigs. I guess this is one of those "do as I say, not as I do" situations. Still, I'll be really surprised if Hitler's SS doesn't show up at some point to save the day, never mind that in 1916 they hadn't even been invented yet.

So, there's four different stories, and they keep jumping back and forth between them in what I assume is an (unsuccessful) attempt to keep us from noticing how boring any single one of them is specifically. The main story is about this old bat who can't get any play from the boys anymore, so she decides to ruin the good times for everyone else. "When women cease to attract men they often turn to Reform as a second choice," the title card explains. Then they show us a bunch of ugly broads! Ha ha! Okay, I'll admit it, that was brilliant. The old bat's meddling ultimately leads to M.A.D.D. stealing some chick's baby after they catch her having one lousy beer with lunch. I swear, if I ever become ~~president~~ king my first course of action will be to declare M.A.D.D. a terrorist organization. Later, a guy is accused of a crime he didn't commit, which leads to a chase between a train and a race car. It's nice to see that lame-ass clichés like this were already boring the piss out of people, even though this is only like the third movie ever made.

The secondary stories include one about how much the Jews suck (Ha! I knew we'd get to that.); one about these frogs who can't agree on whether to be Christian or Catholic so they end up stabbing the crap out of each other; and one about some Babylonian fucks, including this guy they call a "two-sword man" but then they show him and he's only carrying one sword. Oh, wait, I get it.

Needless to say, this shit's all over the place, and a bunch more characters show up too, including Jesus, although he doesn't do anything very important except go on that famous beer run. That's right, Jesus Christ himself is in this movie, but the plot is so complicated and jam-packed with pretentious that he isn't even particularly noticeable. At least we know who he is though - half the clowns in this movie don't even have names! They all go by shit like "Brown Eyes" or "Mountain Girl" (fucking hippie) or "the little Dear One." Okay, no joke here, if I ever met a bitch who answered to "the Dear One" I'd punch her in the hooter immediately, just on general principles. Seriously, fuck the Dear One.

On the flip side, there is a dude they call the "Musketeer of the Slums." Now there's a title to embrace: "Who am I? I'm the Musketeer of the Slums, you trick-ass bitch. Now take off your panties." There's also some riots, which are always a hoot, and a massacre... Oh, and a war. That's right, this flick is so long and tedious that I almost forgot that there's an entire war in it. In fact, now that I look back on it, there might have been a couple. Even with all this violence though this movie still sucks, especially when they come to their big conclusion about intolerance:

"When cannon and prison bars wrought in the fires of intolerance -"

What? That not only makes zero sense, it's not even a complete sentence! You fucking idiots. As awful as this flick is though, apparently it's better than the novelization. I say this because when the title cards in this movie come up sometimes they show "the book of the play" in the background, and if you look really closely you can see that it's just the exact same page repeated over and over! Talk about a fucking ripoff. If they sent me that shit as my Book of the Month Club automatic selection I'd sue everybody.

Suggested Alternative: Legally changing your name to "The Musketeer of the Slums"

#56

King Kong

(1933)
Adventure

Here's an actual conversation I heard at the Wal-Mart the other day:

KID: "Dad, what's 'King Kong'?"
DAD: "He's a big monkey who breaks everything."

That pretty much says it all. But even though it's mustier than your Great Aunt Bertha's snatch, this movie kicks a surprising amount of ass. There's dinosaurs, giant monsters fighting, one of the hottest actresses in history running around with half her clothes torn off, and an enormous amount of property damage. The special effects are pretty old-school, but it doesn't even matter because somehow it just makes everything seem that much more like one of those fucked-up dreams you occasionally have where it all makes sense at the time and you just totally go with it. Except when *King Kong* is over, you don't have to wash your sheets.

There are some minor sticking points, of course. Like when

they're all being chased and eaten by the brontosaurus (a kind of dinosaur that not only didn't eat meat, but, as it turns out, didn't even exist), why does one sailor stop and climb a tree? Did he feel like he'd be safer if he got closer to the dinosaur's mouth? The big problem with this flick though is that all the best stuff is in the middle. The beginning is okay because there's like anticipation or whatever, but for a good time nothing beats tooling around an island full of killer dinosaurs, unless it's tooling around an island full of killer dinosaurs while you're drunk. Once they get King Kong back to New York City though it's all anticlimactic and shit. That's why the Jack Black remake was 4 hours long, and 3 hours and fifty-five minutes of that went down on Dinosaur Island. The cats who made that version knew the score.

Where they really punked the monkey though was by not immediately making a bunch of sequels where King Kong fights other monsters. Instead, they puked up *Son of Kong* (1933), where they find a baby King Kong that becomes the main guy's best friend and helps him solve mysteries. I'm surprised Son of Kong didn't learn to play sports and help win a "the big game" too. Give me a christing break.

Suggested Alternative: *King Kong vs. Godzilla* (1962)

#55

The Magnificent Ambersons

(1942)

Drama

Oh, no... this starts with a bunch of nostalgia. I hate nostalgia. Yeah, yeah, yeah, things were *so* much better back in the day, you like that old time-a rock 'n roll, blah blah blah. Shut up, oldster, I'm trying to watch a movie here.

As you can probably guess, this movie is about the Ambersons, a bunch of snobby, cowardly, whiny, obnoxious, annoying, yachting-type douchebags who hold snooty dances, have relatives named "Aunt Fannie," consider "donating millions to charity" a career, and take sleigh rides with the girls they're planning to rape. So why are they "magnificent?" Because they're rich and white, obviously. Duh.

The trouble begins when one of the no-good Amberson kids, who spent most of his childhood getting into fights because his parents dressed him like Little Lord Faggot-Boy, comes back from asshole finishing school. As befits someone who grew up wearing his hair like Dennis the Menace's girlfriend Margaret, he has some serious mommy issues, and when his dad kicks off

115

and mom starts seeing someone else he flips out and tries to put a stop to it. Everyone yells and pouts and sits in the dark reading heartfelt letters explaining someone else's position, until finally an airplane falls on their house and kills every last one of them. At least that's what I was hoping would happen. What really happens is that the mom tries to placate the son by taking a trip around the world with him.[9]

I'm not sure how long they're supposed to be gone, but the son drags it out as long as possible and it seems like years. Of course it seems like years since I started watching this movie too, so who can say? Naturally mom's boyfriend shows up the second they get back (he must be pretty horny by now), but no one will let him see her and that's the end of that. In the end the mom dies, Aunt Fannie loses all of their remaining money investing in junk bonds, the asshole son gets both his legs jacked up in a car wreck, and I laugh my ass off. Stupid honkies.

Suggested Alternative: *The Abominable Dr. Phibes* (1971)

---

9 This is the type of shit rich people always do to relax, sort of the millionaire version of chugging a six-pack and then decking your brother-in-law.

#54

Rear Window

(1954)
Thriller

I love the magazine the main guy in this movie works for - the cover of the issue in his apartment says "In this issue... Special Report on Europe." That crazy Europe. What has it gotten up to now?

The whole MacGuffin the main guy ends up embroiled in begins because he's stuck in his apartment with a broken leg and decides to start spying on the neighbors.[10] The blonde hottie he peeps at for a while is pretty fine (I wouldn't mind putting something in her rear window), but the real story begins when, based on completely circumstantial evidence, he gets it into his head that the cat in the apartment across the courtyard has murdered his wife. It's basically the same type of conclusion some nosy old busybody with a dried-up twat would jump to, but nobody would pay to see a movie about a meddling old bat like that, especially if a similar bat has ever

---

10 Okay, I realize that not everybody had cable in 1954, but if this guy is that fucking bored why doesn't he have his girl bring him some comic books or something?

called the cops on you for a crime you didn't even commit. (*Intent* to distribute narcotics? Give me a fucking break.) That's why this movie tries to make the story more palatable by replacing the busybody with a regular guy. Oh, and the fact that he turns out to be right helps, too. (Then again, he calls his cop buddy multiple times about this supposed murder, but when it looks like a different neighbor is about to commit suicide he just shrugs it off and lets her go about her business. I think that definitively pegs him as more of a busybody than a humanitarian.)

Motives aside, this movie has a reputation for being all suspenseful and shit, but truth be told nothing really happens until the last half hour; the rest of it is just a bunch of boring filler. If you ask me, Alfred Hitchcock Presents probably should've saved this one for his TV show. Right about the time most people are fighting to stay awake, the main guy's girl finally decides to sneak into the killer's crib and, wouldn't you know it, just then the killer comes back, leaving the main guy to watch helplessly while she possibly gets skewered. That's right, I said *helplessly*. "Handi-capable" my ass.

Now, supposedly this final bit is a serious classic of suspense, but don't be fooled - the reason it's retarded is staring you right in the face. Think about it: it's broad daylight, and the entire movie is based on the fact that twenty different neighbors can see and hear *everything* that goes on in the entire complex. The whole building can hear the killer's phone ringing for fuck's sake, so I'm sure they'd hear a bunch of screaming and murdering. It's not like the main guy's girl is in any real danger, even though he goes through all these over-the-top histrionics pretending that she is. Or, to break out the fancy guest words, the whole premise automatically invalidates itself.

And then there's the very end, where Captain Wheelchair holds the killer off with a flashbulb. Why doesn't the killer dude just close his eyes and rush the main guy's crippled ass? I mean, if he's reduced to defending himself with a camera it's a pretty safe bet he isn't packing a gun. The only thing even more absurd is after the killer *does* bum rush the main guy and everyone comes running out of their apartments, sped-up Benny Hill style, to find him hanging from his window, in his huge-ass cast, flailing around like a complete spasmo. It's like something that would happen to the Three Stooges. I'm not kidding, it's a laugh riot.

Better luck next time, Hitch.

Suggested Alternative: *Disturbia* (2007)

#53

The Passion of Joan of Arc

(1928)

Drama

This Joan of the Lost Arc is nowhere near as hot as the one in *Bill & Ted's Excellent Adventure* (1988). How am I supposed to root for her if she isn't a least a little hot? And that's not all they skimp on - this has to be one of the cheapest-looking movies around. There's almost nothing in any of the rooms the story plays out in except for a satanic chicken drawn on one wall. It's like they fired the set designer at the last minute and replaced him with someone's pissed-off 13-year-old nephew who listens to too much death metal.

The story is about the time they put Joan of the Arc on trial for cross-dressing and blowing the Devil. Or whatever. Apparently the prerequisites for being in on this trial are sporting ridiculous hair or wearing a funny hat, but don't let the fact that they look like a bunch of goons fool you, because they've got the stack decked against Ms. Arc. Not that it was really necessary, since her entire defense consists of staring off into space like a crazy person and giving answers that are either total nonsense or completely batshit insane.

Of course next to nothing actually happens. They do threaten to torture Joan at one point, but unfortunately this turns out to be a bluff. I guess it was too much to hope that this movie would turn into a depraved, torture porn classic like *Make Them Die Slowly* (1981) or *The Passion of the Christ* (2004).

In the end most of this flick is just a mediocre chick crying, and if I enjoyed watching that I'd punch my girlfriend's BFF. In fact, they're so desperate to slip something marketable into this movie that in one part there's a completely pointless scene of a baby sucking on a tit, just to get a tit in there and land that R rating. Oh well, at least the end is intense - the prosecution decides to burn Joan at the stake (I guess she didn't realize that the *stakes* were so high! Ha ha!), and they actually show the bitch cooking while all her supporters riot. It might have served their cause a little better if they had rioted *before* their girl was set on fire, but better late then never. I guess.

Incidentally, I have no idea why this movie is called "The PASSION of Joan of Arc." She doesn't fuck anybody.

Suggested Alternative: I'm gonna have to go with Bill & Ted

■■■■■■■

#52

■■■■■■■

North By Northwest

(1959)
Thriller

No matter how good a movie is, there's always some pain-in-the-ass who will find a bunch of nit-picky things wrong with it. I hate people like that. I bring this up because lots of folks will tell you that this movie's plot doesn't necessarily make a whole lot of sense, but if you ask me they're totally missing the point. Alfred Hitchcock Presents movies aren't about the big picture, they're more about all the little things that happen along the way. Think about it, this is the guy who invented the word *MacGuffin,* which is defined as "some bullcrap excuse for everyone in a movie to run around fighting and doing cool shit." For example:

- In this flick, these cats want to kill the main guy because of mistaken identity, so they get him shitfaced and then put him behind the wheel of a car. Frankly I call that "being a good host." As far as murder plots go it's strictly amateur hour. The fact that he manages to escape and then gets busted for drunk driving is pretty hilarious, though. I love it when movies play drunk driving for laughs. Because it's funny.

- The main guy is talking to this other dude when one of the bad guys ninjas a knife right into the other dude's back. Not one of the thirty people standing two feet away sees this go down of course, so the main guy grabs the knife handle, poses with the dead dude so that it looks like *he* stabbed him, waits for everyone to notice, pulls the knife out of his back, pauses for a photo op with it, then drops it and runs away. Frankly he does everything he can think of to look as guilty as possible except confess on live TV while fucking the dead cat's wife. It's the clumsiest, most inane set-up for a misunderstanding in movie history. Ol' Alfred Hitchcock Presents should've studied episodes of *Three's Company* until he learned how to do this shit right.

- The bad guys' next plan to put the main guy out of commission is to lure him somewhere in the general vicinity of halfway to no place and then chase him down with a crop duster. At first I thought they were actually gonna crop dust him in an attempt to give him some sort of upper respiratory infection, which might take a while to kill him but I suppose would get the job done eventually. But no, they try to shoot him in a full-on airplane drive-by. Wouldn't it have been easier to do this from a car? Or hell, they tricked him into thinking that he was gonna meet someone out there, so can't the person he meets just walk up and shoot him? Why'd they have to go and make things so complicated?

- The thrilling climax involves a chase across Mt. Rushmore. This is kind of cool in theory, but as it turns out it's impossible to take an action scene seriously when your main guy is hanging from a giant nose. I can't believe this wasn't blatantly obvious while they were filming this part. To be fair, it probably was, but I suppose once you've built the giant nose you're pretty much committed.

I could go on, but I think I've proved my point. Whatever the hell it was.

On an unrelated note, I had the closed captions on while I was watching this (the skirt I was fucking at the time was making a lot of racket), and I noticed that there weren't just subtitles when characters talked, but when they wrote things down, too. Is that for the benefit of people who are blind *and* deaf but still want to watch this movie?

Suggested Alternative: *Frenzy* (1972)

🎞️🎞️🎞️🎞️

#51

🎞️🎞️🎞️🎞️

The Deer Hunter
(1978)
Drama

You know those people who live in one place for their entire lives, work in factories, know how to fix their own cars, and drink beverages out of cans? Well, this flick is about them. And, naturally, they all end up going to Vietnam. I swear, you'd think Vietnam was the only war we ever fought.

Before we even get there though there's an endless wedding scene that's longer than any real wedding I've ever been to and at least one marriage I can think of. Seriously, we couldn't have burned through the wedding in like ten minutes and gotten on with it? I mean hell, they show us everything except the part where a bunch of assholes do the "Chicken Dance." If I ever get married again I swear to fuck the "Chicken Dance" is fully *verboten.* Also "YMCA." Things do pick up when everyone finally gets to the 'Nam – there's women and children exploded, a guy cooked alive, and some torture – but before long we're back home, listening to everyone whine about it. You know, it really could've been a lot fucking worse, Vietnam vets. You could've been one of those people who got out of it by moving to Canada.

Of course the whining goes on forever, but the ironic part is that, in the long run, the wedding, Vietnam, and even the whining don't really matter - it's all just window dressing for what's basically the *Rocky* of Russian roulette movies! Okay, fine, the *Over the Top* (1987) of Russian roulette movies. But seriously, could someone please tell me where the hell *that* came from? And more importantly, why isn't there a Kenny Loggins song on the soundtrack to illustrate it? I'm relatively certain Kenny Loggins had been invented by 1978, much to the world's chagrin. Now *there's* something to whine about.

Suggested Alternative: *Bambi* (1942)

#50

Greed

(1924)
Drama

"Personally directed by Erich Von Stroheim." The ego on this guy, right?

True story: My buddy Juan used to have an actual *film* copy of this that he salvaged from his parents' failing Mexican movie theater just before they burned it down for the insurance money. We threaded it up and watched some of it once, but the damn thing was *six hours long* and boring as piss so we took all 33 reels and used them to wrap his neighbor's entire outhouse in film. The poor bastard had to cut through it with a machete before he could take a crap! It was fucking hilarious.

My point being, I'm secretly kind of glad that I was only able to track down the short version this time.

It starts with the main guy picking up an injured bird and putting it into his mouth. Doesn't he know that's how you get bird rabies? Stupid asshole. He takes the little bird with him so he can nurse it back to health and they can solve mysteries together, but then this raging prick smacks the bird right out of his hands! The main guy loses it, picks the asshole up over his head, and throws him off a bridge! Oh, and did I mention that this all goes down at work? Nowadays the main guy would probably get a raise out of fear that he would sue the company for the pulled muscle he incurred when he lifted that dude over his head, but this is the (good) old days so he just gets shit-canned. Fortunately the phony roadshow dentist just happens to be in town, and our main guy is able to hook up with him. Of course every parent wants their kid to learn a fraudulent trade, but main guy's mom is still so sad when he goes off into the world that she eats her handkerchief.

Years go by and now our hero is an unlicensed, misogynist dentist in San Francisco. Oh, and he lets his employees run some illegal gambling on the side. The American dream. One day one of his patients brings in his "incest is best" cousin/girlfriend for some dental work, and the main guy starts crushing on her in a big way. He hedges his bets by kissing her while she's gassed out in the dental chair, but then he asks her out legitimately and pretty soon he's filling *all* her cavities. Their dates aren't much to speak of...

CHICK: "Let's go over and sit on the sewer."

...but I suppose that's appropriate for an incest slut who used to fuck her own cousin and a dentist who sexually molests his patients. Except the phrase is "*in* the sewer."

Eventually these two degenerates get engaged and then, within *hours,* the chick just *happens* to win the illegal lottery run out of her new fiance's office. How fucking convenient. The good times don't last long though - someone turns the main guy in for dentisting without a license, so he's reduced to roaming the streets in the rain, looking for work. Pretty soon he's giving the Mrs. the ol' Vulcan nerve pinch and slapping her around for booze money, and she's cutting corners by feeding him week-old meat most people wouldn't give to the dog. The wife sits on that lottery money like it's made of gold though - I think she even strips down to her underwear at night and rolls around in it like a kinky Scrooge McDuck. Finally the main guy flips a gasket and beats her to within an inch of her life, but unfortunately for him it's an inch in the wrong direction and now he's wanted for murder. He tries to escape by disguising himself as a singing cowboy's gruff but trusty sidekick, but that doesn't fool anybody and, ultimately, he comes to a bad end. Just like this movie. Except if you ask me this boring-ass movie has a bad beginning and a bad middle too.

Suggested Alternative: *Brewster's Millions* (1985)

#49

The Bicycle Thief

(1948)

Drama

Besides the thief mentioned in the title, there's also a psychic and some Christians in this movie, and they're *all* Italian. It's an endless parade of crooks!

The story, such as it is, begins when this dirt-poor sack who's been looking for work finally lands his idea of a sweet gig: plastering posters that no one will read all over town. Just like your band used to do, remember? He needs a bicycle though, so he and the Mrs. go down to the pawn shop and hock their sheets to buy one. Good enough, but on the way home his numb-cunt wife just has to visit the psychic she's been squandering their money on behind his back. If I found out that my wife was wasting valuable bread like that she wouldn't need a psychic because she'd already know what her future held: a legendary ass-beating, followed by a mysterious disappearance.

Luckily for this broad the main guy is so happy about his new career that he doesn't even care, but then, on his very first day, someone steals his new bike! Amazingly enough it isn't a black kid, but that's neither here nor there because now he's out one bike *and* one job and he can't even go home and cry into his pillow because his wife probably hocked that to pay the cable bill. He does report the theft to the pigs, but the cop he tells his story to gets called away to the nuclear celery meeting and you know how those drag on, so he has no choice but to look for the bike himself.

Our hero rounds up the Get-Along-Gang and they start by looking for his bike at the open-air ~~thief~~ flea market, but you know Italians: there's so many stolen bikes to sort through that it's totally hopeless. Finally he's so desperate that *he* goes to the psychic. Stupid asshole; you've already been ripped off once today. And I hate to point out the obvious, but he already *got* the address of the cat who might have his bike in a scene just prior to this! I guess the movie temporarily forgot its own plot or something. The address doesn't pan out anyway, but eventually the main guy just randomly bumps into the thief! The bike's long gone by this point though and he can't prove squat, so even ridiculous plot contrivances won't help him now. In the end he tries to steal someone else's bike, but he gets caught. Wouldn't this movie have made a better, way more cynical point if he had gotten away with it? I guess it doesn't really matter because either way the whole story's completely retarded. Seriously dude, just take the bus.

Suggested Alternative: *Reality Bites* (1995)

(Incidentally, does anybody wanna buy a bike?)

```
▯▯▯▯▯▯▯▯
```
#48
```
▯▯▯▯▯▯▯▯
```

Double Indemnity

(1944)
Thriller

Speaking of bottom-feeding, thieving scumbags, the main guy in this flick is an insurance salesman. Seriously, don't you love how insurance – which is basically gambling, at sucker odds, against someone who won't pay up if you win – is completely legal no matter how blatantly the insurance companies rip everyone off, but the second someone rips them off it's such a horrific crime that even the movies find it morally justifiable for the person in question to end up getting shot and dying a lingering death on their way to jail? Okay, fine, so the scam artists in this particular movie murdered a guy too, but I'm sure you can see what I'm getting at.

The indemnity begins when the main guy, a lonely widower with three sons to feed, decides to solve both his problems by helping this dame kill her husband and collect on the insurance in exchange for some of the money and all of her pussy. Frankly I'm surprised she's willing to play ball with him at all, given the laughable pass he makes at her the first time they meet: "Suppose you do this... suppose I do that... suppose some other stupid-ass comment..." Suppose you shut the fuck up until you get some actual game, idiot? Seriously, that was just embarrassing. Hell, even the dame's maid is operating at a zero respect level at this point:

INSURANCE AGENT: "Where would the living room be?"
MAID: "In there. But they keep the liquor locked up."

Ha! Good on her.

So here's the plan these two clowns cook up: first they ice the husband, then the main guy impersonates him, gets on a train, and pretends to fall off, after which they leave the dead body on the tracks. It's deceptively complicated. For someone trying to commit the perfect murder the main guy isn't very concerned about leaving fingerprints all over everything though - he touches the body, the dead guy's hat, his crutches... I'm surprised he didn't jerk off all over the scene and put one of his business cards in the corpse's pocket while he was at it.

Not that it matters either way because the whole scheme is ridiculous and before long it's pretty obvious that the jig is up. Or the gig is up. Whichever. Nevertheless, this doesn't sway the dame from pulling out a gun and plugging the main guy. I guess she figures that if you're gonna go down for life you might as well go down for the whole enchilada. The main guy does manage to survive long enough to record a full confession though, and I have to say... what a windbag. He couldn't just say "It was me," or "My bad," or something?

Poor planning aside, this all may sound sufficiently badass, but trust me, it's not, mainly because they don't actually show any of the good stuff, like the husband being snuffed, or even the main guy boning the weird-looking (but strangely hot) wife.

They should've called it "Double Lame-demity."

Suggested Alternative: *The Woman in the Window* (1944)

#47

MASH

(1970)
Comedy

You know, if fucking *MASH* can make this list, then there's no reason why *Caddyshack* or *King Frat* shouldn't be on here too. Seriously, here's just some of the juvenile shit that goes down in this movie:

- A guy manufactures a zany misunderstanding solely as an excuse to steal a jeep.
- Everybody gets a sexist nickname, unless they're a dude. Then they get a racist one.
- Two of the main guys put the kibosh on this underage kid's Bible study so he has more time to fix them martinis. They also give him porn.
- Someone puts a microphone under the bed while an uptight chick is getting boned senseless and broadcasts it over the entire camp.
- Everybody rides the Christian cat so hard that he finally flips out and ends up in the crazyhouse.
- A couple of guys want to know if the uptight chick's

throw rug matches her blinds, so they expose her naked in front of everybody.

- A no-nonsense, by-the-book tool is knocked out and photographed with Asian hookers.

Plus boozing, fighting, gambling, womanizing, authority defying, blasphemy, dick jokes, gay jokes, drug abuse, gore, tits, and one of the best football games ever filmed, for you ass-patters who are into that. My favorite thing about this flick though? Nurse Storch. You probably don't even know who Nurse Storch is unless you watch this movie every day while dressed as one of the characters, but you should definitely pay attention next time it's on AMC or something because trust me, she's incredible. God *damn* do I want the fuck out of that. It really is too bad that more people remember the corny, idiot TV series – with all its moronic sitcom one-liners and preachy, unearned sentiment – because this flick legitimately kicks ass. Here's something you probably didn't know though: there were three *other* TV shows based on this movie: *AfterMASH* (1983-1984); *Trapper John, M.D.* (1979-1986); and *W*A*L*T*E*R* (1984). Fun fact: All of these shows sucked.

Suggested Alternative: *Stripes* (1981)

#46

L'Advventura

(1960)
Drama

Jesus H., didn't I just watch this? Oh, wait, that was *L'Atalante*. *Pardon* fucking *moi*.

Early on in this flick some people are tooling their boats around just adjacent to the middle of nowhere when one of them says that she saw a shark. Not long after, they're all roaming around this uninhabited island when one girl disappears, and later still two people looking for the missing girl come upon this mysterious, abandoned town that overlooks a huge cemetery. That makes three separate instances where it looks like this is going to turn into a horror movie, but it never does. Stop yanking my rod, *L'Advventura*.

The rest of the movie is about the missing girl's fiance, who, after she disappears, wastes zero time rectifying the situation. But which I mean he hooks up with her BFF immediately. Not that I really blame the guy. I mean, missing girl isn't super hideous or anything, but she is sporting the mole to end all moles smack dab in the middle of her forehead, and frankly it would be a bit much to have to look at over breakfast every morning. For real, this chick could've done her scenes topless and I wouldn't have even noticed because that thing was like a magnet for your eyes. She's probably the first girl in history who's tired of saying "My eyes are *down* here!"

So anyway, missing girl's friends do scour the island looking for her, and so do the police, but since they haven't invented the mole detector yet they never do find the bitch. The fiance and BFF literally have nothing better to do though, so they decide to drive all over Europe and see if she turns up.

Now, I don't want to give the impression that everything that happens from this point on is just completely random, but yes I do: they watch some sketchy weasel throw spit at a fat chick; the main guy ruins this kid's sketch for no reason and when the kid wants to fight the main guy acts all been-there, done-that as a roundabout way of punking out; and in one part they visit a nun factory and ring the bells without permission, which I'm pretty sure you're not supposed to do because doesn't ringing religious bells generally signal something important? Everyone within hearing range probably thought that it was the Rapture. Or, you know, lunchtime or something.

In the end the main guy finally gets bored with all of this (I can definitely sympathize), blows off the BFF, and hooks up with girl #3. Kinda dickish, but hey, he's traded up every time so good on him. When the BFF catches him with his new(est) squeeze she runs off crying, which is SCB (Standard Chick Behavior), but for some reason he chases her down and then he ends up crying too. At this point I fully expected him to have a complete breakdown and whack the skirt and that would be the big twist. You know, like he killed the first girl all along because his whole angle is to kiss the girls and make 'em die. That doesn't happen though and the movie just ends, which I think perfectly illustrates the difference between regular movies and artistic ones. In regular movies, you're supposed to be impressed when you find out what everything has been building up to. In artistic ones, you're supposed to be impressed when it doesn't build up to anything at all.

Suggested Alternative: *Island of Death* (1977)

🎞️ ▯▯▯▯▯▯▯

#45

🎞️ ▯▯▯▯▯▯▯

The Searchers

(1956)
Western

John Wayne again? God damn it. This time around he's proud of one thing and one thing only: fightin' for the South. (Black people can probably turn this movie off right now.) If there's one thing he hates more than the nigs though it's the fucking Injuns, so when they push his buttons by slaughtering half his family and kidnapping the rest, he goes after 'em with both guns blazing and some additional guns besides. He's so furious that he even shoots this dead Indian's eyes out, in the hopes that it will make him blind in Indian heaven or something. Really, you can't get much more pissed off than that.

Five years later he *finally* tracks down the only survivor, his niece, but then she tells him to blow because she wants to stay with the Indians! Ha ha! Now he's beyond livid, especially after the dude he's riding with (who's literally a dude in this case) stops him from shooting the bitch. He manages to maintain until they get back home though, where they work out their frustrations by busting up a wedding. They decide to rein it in when they find out that they're both wanted for murder (due to some previous transpirin's that I didn't bother to mention), but before that's settled some additional circumstances ensue and they get their chance to rescue the niece after all. The end. Oh, wait, the two main guys are still wanted for murder, aren't they? Well, the people who made this movie forgot all about that, so why shouldn't we?

There is some generalized, low-key badassery in the course of this flick, but they make a few pretty stupid assumptions to get some of these bits to work. Example: cowboys can ride their horses through a river, but Indians will fall down like the Three Stooges when they attempt to do the same thing. Even worse, there's a part about halfway through where the good guys are camping out and you can see movie lights and shit over the top of the fake background for the entire scene! Talk about bush league. Frankly the best part of the whole movie is when this fat chick gets rolled down a hill. Roll, fatty, roll! As for John Wayne, once again you can tie-dye me unimpressed. His two big moves throughout the entire running time are being a complete dick and occasionally saying "That'll be the day." What a moron. Hey, John Wayne, are you ever gonna stop chugging cock?

JOHN WAYNE: "That'll be the day."

Suggested Alternative: *Posse* (1993)

#44

Ben-Hur

(1959)
Drama

Heh heh. "Bend Her."

Back when this came out they were making nothing but Bible movies: *The Ten Amendments* (1956); *King of Things* (1961); *The Story of Babe Ruth* (1960); *East of Eden* (1955)... Naturally nobody could stand it, because let's face it, the only things more boring than the Bible are people who are interested in the Bible, and possibly baseball. Well, this flick slipped in through the back door by pretending to be a Bible movie too, but it's laughably obvious that all the Bible shit is just tacked on. Sure, famous Bible people keep popping up like special guest stars on a sweeps week episode of *Sheriff Lobo*, but trust me, you could replace almost every single one of their scenes with a cameo appearance by Bob Hope and it wouldn't make a lick of difference.

The only part where a Bible person actually plays an important role is at the very end, where the main guy's leper relatives (everybody's got a couple, am I right?) come out of hiding to

142

see that Bible guy who had the leprosy miracle cure. But even this goes nowhere, because the guy in question is currently being busted for practicing medicine without a license or something, so he's not exactly in any position to see a couple of walk-ins who don't even have insurance. What I don't get though is that he strolls *right by* the lepers at one point and they don't even try to cure themselves by touching the hem of his garment. Don't they ever listen to Sam Cooke? Oh, wait, two minutes later they're spontaneously cured anyway, for no reason whatsoever. Way to respect our intelligence, *Ben-Hur*.

Anyway, the story actually begins long before this, with an argument between this Jewish cat – he's the main guy – and his best friend, who isn't Jewish so we'll call him the main goy. The main guy is a real piece of work: he owns slaves, he brags about how rich he is, and he even tongues down some other cat's fiancee solely because the opportunity presents itself. Karma comes a-calling though when he gets arrested for a crime he didn't commit and his sister only sort-of committed. He tries to make a run for it while they're transferring him to another facility, but they catch him again and he ends up one of those poor saps who has to row a giant boat alongside a hundred other dudes for the rest of his life.

Wow, can you imagine being one of those guys? Every day you'd be like "How the fuck did it come to this?" And the only hilarious workplace gag you had any realistic chance of pulling off – singing "Row, row, row your boat..." – would probably get pretty stale after a while.

Eventually the boat our main guy's been assigned to runs into some trouble and he ends up rescuing this famous rich guy, who decides to pay him back by getting the charges dropped and giving him a fresh start. So, like one of those crippled newspaper boys who moves up the ranks until finally he's getting coffee for the cat who owns the company, our hero gets in good with the establishment and climbs the corporate latter until eventually he's rich enough to go back home and be the bigger man by getting revenge.

Along the way there's a kickass battle between two fleets of toy boats, a bunch of sorry assholes are chained to a ship so they'll drown when it sinks, a huge sword fight between hundreds of guys breaks out, a dude's face is set on fire, two chicks *literally* rot in jail, and ESPN 6 sponsors a wicked chariot race, which is by far the best part of the movie. I love any sporting event that ends with people being trampled to death, which is why, as boring as it is, I'll take soccer over American football any day.

Suggested Alternative: *Life of Brian* (1979)

#43

Battleship Potemkin

(1925)

Drama

Okay, so we've got a battleship, and we've got a potemkin, whatever the hell that it. I think it's some kind of soup. Actually that kind of makes sense, because this story begins on a ship, and everyone knows that you can't be in charge of a ship and just keep pissing everyone off because sooner or later they're gonna have a mutiny and you'll end up sleeping in Davy Jones' or Peter Tork's locker, feeding the octopuses. And it's always something inconsequential that finally sets the riff-raff off too, like serving up a crappy lunch. See, this is where the soup comes in.

So the Russian sailors in this movie mutiny and take over their ship, and things get even worse for the Man when everyone in town takes their side and starts to riot and shit. The people in charge have no choice but to send in the pigs, who start blasting away at everything in sight and chasing people down these stairs which leads to the only real reason this movie is famous, this part where a runaway baby carriage is rolling down the stairs while everyone is shooting all around it. You might remember them stealing this bit for *The Untouchables* (the one from the 1980's, starring the original James Bond and Kevin Costcutter), the only difference being that the 1980's take was so ludicrous and over the top that the day I saw it the entire audience was either so pissed off or laughing so hard that they actually had to stop the movie until order was maintained. In fact, I can pretty much guarantee that if they had run out of popcorn at that exact moment we would have had our own Tsar Wars Russian Revolution on the spot, seized the theater for the People, and used it to actually show important, artistic movies starring foreigners and lesbians. Until six months later, when we went bankrupt and had to go back to booking garbage like *Die Hard 3* (1995).

Getting back to *Battleship Potemkin*, there's like a million different DVDs of it out there, and since it's old, silent, and foreign, every single one has completely different music and subtitles. The music on the version I watched was especially bizarre: sometimes it's dead on (like when the sailors are getting ready for the big battle at the end), sometimes it doesn't match what's happening in the movie at all, and sometimes it sounds like music made with power tools and objects found around the house. They never say who the musicians are though. Maybe 45 Grave.

As for the subtitles, frankly they were pretty suspect. Like after this little kid gets shot and trampled we're supposed to believe that his mom says "My boy is very ill." Yeah, he's got lead poisoning and foot-in-skull disease! Ha ha ha! Or the subtitles will be several sentences long, but what they're translating is just a couple of words, like "театр 6урНые" or whatnot. I'm sorry, but I refuse to believe that Russian is that efficient. Especially since their entire political system collapses every time they forget to pay the electric bill or something.

Suggested Alternative: *Battlestar Galactica* (1978)

#42

From Here to Eternity

(1953)

Drama

Why is everyone always giving Ben Affleck such a hard time? I mean, he made this same movie in 2001 (*Pearl Harbor*) and movie critics ruptured their sphincters in their rush to shit all over it. But drop Sheriff Lobo and the fat guy from *The Black Hole* (1979) into the exact same story and suddenly it's the greatest movie ever made. Okay, fine, the 42nd greatest. But that's still pretty good.

You know what would make it a lot better though? If they tweaked it so we could enjoy all the explosions and violence at the end in glorious color. I know it looked pretty crummy when they tried colorizing black & white movies in the 1980's, but for some reason the only colors they had available back then were the kind that "glow in black light." You know, like those Led Zeppelin posters your uncle has in his garage. With computers the way they are nowadays I'm sure they could to do way a better job. Maybe they could Photoshop Ben Affleck in there too. If you ask me, the guy deserves a break.

And it's not like he could do much damage, since nothing important happens in this flick until the very end anyway. In fact, the military guys in this movie wouldn't know important if they stepped on it and it blew both their legs off. Their entire schedule consists of doling out petty work details in an attempt to force some clown to join the boxing team, trying to get promotions for the sole purpose of being in the position to bone someone else's wife, ditching out on guard duty to get drunk, and, naturally, training all day and all night to walk in unison. You know, like the Smurfs.

Is it really any surprise that the dirty Japs were able to so thoroughly bushwhack us?

Suggested Alternative: *Tora! Tora! Tora!* (1970)

#41

8½

(1963)
Gibberish

At first I assumed this would be a movie about a really good-looking girl. You know, like *10* (1979), except this particular chick isn't quite as hot. Instead, it's another goddamned movie about some asshole making a movie. I said it before and I'll say it again: making a movie about making a movie is like jerking off to a picture of yourself jerking off. Even worse, this guy isn't even making the damn thing yet - he's just hanging around trying to come up with an *idea* for his movie! What's truly obnoxious though is that every once in a while someone in *this* movie will straight-up point out how meaningless it all is! That's right, the guy who made this pile is actually rubbing our faces in the fact that watching it is a complete waste of time! Seriously, you miserable cocksucker, why didn't you just film yourself flipping us off for two hours?

To be fair, exactly one of his go-nowhere ideas is kinda cool, and it's the very first scene in the movie, which, now that you know this, should save you a lot of time. The rest of them are just plain boring though, or shit that no one wants to see, like a morbidly fat chick with dirty hair dancing the Rumba. Here's some other stupid crap our main guy considers making his motionless picture about:

- His dead father, who probably killed himself to avoid watching his son's movies.
- A little kid dressed as Kato running away from some priests and then getting loads of Catholic guilt from his mom. For not letting them catch and rape him, I guess.
- Having his own harem. Now here's an idea with some potential; too bad the lion's share of the chicks in this part are hideous beyond belief. Which is why they're the ones that I would throw to the lion.

Speaking of hideous chicks, could someone please explain to me why this jackass has a bim on the side who's uglier and more annoying than his actual wife? I think you're a little unclear on the concept, idiot. Naturally the wife busts them at one point and a long, half-hearted argument ensues, because that's just what this awful, obtuse, dull, go-nowhere movie needed - a bunch of petty bickering. Christ.

Remember when your 7th grade teacher explained that you should never, never, never, under any circumstances, write about how you can't think of anything to write about because that's the oldest, lamest cop-out in the book and it totally identifies you as a talentless, grade-A hack? Case closed.

Suggested Alternative: *Un Chien Andalou* (1929)

□□□□□□□

#40

□□□□□□□□

Mr. Smith Goes to Washington

(1939)

Drama

Hey, Baby Dumpling is in this movie! I know "Baby Dumpling" sounds like a puppet from some Christian television show or something, but he was actually an actor who got saddled with that handle as a baby and ended up stuck with it until the day he died. Can you imagine how many fights he got into over the course of a lifetime? Thinking about that always makes me smile.

Now, initially I thought that this was the movie starring Ronald Reagan and the monkey, but it turns out that one's called "Bedtime for Bob Dole" or something. This movie is actually about a shady political cat named "Big Jim,"[11] who's scheming to buy up all this land where some dam is gonna be built. (Big Jim and Jughead in "Dam Scam.") The crooked senator who's in on the whole thing croaks though, so Big Jim and his crew have to bring in a new senator to be their stooge.

It seems like they're on the ball at first because the guy they

11 All shady political cats are named "Big Jim."

pick appears to be mildly retarded, but as it turns out he doesn't take shit from anybody. When a bunch of reporters make a fool out of him, for example, he tracks down every single one of them and kicks their asses! Even worse for the bad guys, their new pet senator is into little boys (heh), and he wants to set up a boys' camp right where their underhanded shenanigans are transpiring.

Looks like it's time to arrange an "accidental" shooting, and frankly I doubt the main guy would even be missed seeing as no one even seems to know what state he's supposed to be senator of. Somehow, the bad guys never think of that though. Instead, they try to distract him with pussy. That doesn't work for long (little boys, remember), so finally they just frame him. It looks like he's finished, but then this chick talks him into fighting back so at the next senator meeting he does one of those filibuster things where a senator is allowed to talk for as long as he wants, about absolutely anything, as long as he doesn't stop or sit down.

This is a little off the subject, but I just came up with a great idea: a Washington D.C.-based fast food chain that sells a burger called the "Filibuster Bellybuster." The ad campaign could go something like this: "If you really want that senator to stop talking, put *this* in his mouth!" Franchise opportunities are totally available. Contact me.

Anyway, in real life most Americans don't even know that we have a senate much less care what it does, but this is an especially naive and corny movie so naturally the main guy's speech wreaks utter chaos: adults are smacking around little kids, demonstrations are being fire-hosed by the pigs, trucks are running each other off the road... It's laughable beyond belief. Finally, in an effort to get him to stop, one dude brings in thousands of telegrams and letters from the anti-main guy coalition begging him to please shut the fuck up. Now if I was in the main guy's shoes I'd have been like "Well, okay. I guess we better read every single one of these," just to see the look of total despair on the other senators' faces. But does the main guy do something hilarious like that? Nope. Instead, he passes out! And after only 24 hours, too. What a pussy.

Suggested Alternative: Mr. Satanism goes to the lavatory

#39

The Rules of the Game

(1939)
Drama

1) No teeth.
2) The carpet is hot lava. If you touch the carpet, all your clothes get burned off.
3) You can bring a friend, but only if she weighs less than you.

Oh, wait, wrong rules. Uh, forget you just read that, okay?

A guy flies solo across the Atlantic to impress some broad, although I can't imagine why seeing as she's an utter hag with awful hair who dresses like Little Orphan Annie. Seriously, you could scrounge up a better piece in that mysterious, locked shed behind the crooked nursing home.

Bitch doesn't give a flying fuck what this clown does anyway;[12] she can't even be bothered to meet him when he lands because she's too busy playing with a racist music box and listening to her whore assistant prattle on and on about cheating on her

12 Heh. "Flying fuck." Get it?

husband. Later both these dumb sluts, the pilot, and an assortment of other inbred assholes all visit this country estate, where they do a bunch of lame, rich people shit like hunting pheasant, acting world-weary and above it all ("Sincere people are such bores."), putting on a little show that's so annoying and douchey that I actually wished I was there so I could slit every throat in the place, throwing a masquerade ball, and just generally pissing me off.

There's no real story, just ugly people cheating on each other, the girliest fistfight I've ever seen, a slapstick chase, a pissed-off husband waving a gun around, and the previously-mentioned hag trying to mount anything that's longer than it is wide. All this might have been tolerable if the chicks were hot and/or we saw them naked, but they're mostly not and we totally don't. Ultimately, watching this flick is like spending a weekend someplace horrible, with people you hate, and not even getting laid out of the deal. Which I can do on my own, thank you very much.

The only thing I did like about this movie was that it all built up to a lame-brained, convoluted, and completely-avoidable tragedy. Don't get me wrong, the ending is utterly contrived (there's less mistaken identity in *North By Northwest*), and I'm not claiming it's actually good or anything. I was just happy to see someone get shot.

Suggested Alternative: *The Discreet Charm of the Bourgeoisie* (1972)

#38

Bonnie and Clyde

(1967)

Drama

Excellent, a crime spree. I love crime sprees, especially when they're more-or-less directionless. It's like jazz. This movie is about legendary crooks Clyde Barrow and Bonnie Tyler, and if you know your history like I do then you know that the original Bonnie was pretty damn fine. She was like the "Foxy Knoxy" of her generation. Too bad this movie's version of Clyde can't get it up, which totally precludes any wild sex scenes. Even without any sex though we've still got auto theft, bank robbery, pig-capping, people shot in the face, shit busted up, folks being kidnapped, grenades lobbed at the cops, car chases, and, best of all, the first time we see Bonnie you can definitely eyeball some nipple if you really pay attention. There are a few, isolated parts that are kind of dumb (what's with Clyde's brother thinking that a mattress will stop a bullet?), but overall this flick manages to be pretty badass, and it will undoubtedly inspire moronic couples who think they're in love to knock over liquor stores for years to come.

Suggested Alternative: *Gun Crazy* (1950)

#37

Taxi Driver

(1976)
Drama

I really don't understand why people like this movie so much. Don't get me wrong, it has a great, gory ending, but other than that it's just a bunch of putzing around. I mean, you've got this guy...

What? Yeah, as a matter of fact I *am* talking to you. Shut the fuck up, faggot.

So you've got this guy. He drives his cab around for a while, asks some girl out, takes her to a porno movie on their first date,[13] half-heartedly stalks her, buys some guns, works out,[14] foils a robbery, gets a mohawk (fucking poser, I'll bet he doesn't own a single Exploited album), half-assedly tries to assassinate Senator Palpatine... Come the fuck on, this isn't all that different from my week. Rest assured, not one second of

---

13 Stupid asshole, you're supposed to save that for the third date. That way you have something to whack it to if she doesn't put out.

14 Once again proving he's a total moron. You don't have to be in shape if you own a bunch of guns. That's the whole reason one owns a bunch of guns in the first place.

this is the least bit interesting.

And what in hell's fuck is with the Care Bears-inspired happy ending??? In the thrilling climax the main guy goes ballistic, gorily murders three people in front of this little girl, and gets shot twice in the process, once in the neck, but then we're supposed to buy that it all works out just fine for everyone??? The main guy doesn't die from that hole in his neck? No charges are pressed even though he killed those people in cold blood? No one sues him? The little girl doesn't wake up screaming every night for at least the rest of her life? Her parents don't go broke paying for all the therapy? Give me a fucking break. What a load of Hollywood horseshit.

I think the TV show *Taxi* (1978-1983) was based on this movie. If it wasn't, it should've been. BLAM! BLAM! BLAM! Take that, Andy Kaufman, you irritating, overrated fuck.

Suggested Alternative: *DC Cab* (1983)

#36

Dr. Strangelove or: How I Learned to Stop Worrying and Love the Bomb

(1964)

Comedy

This flick is all about making fun of the Cold War, which means it's about as irrelevant today as any given James Bond movie, with the added minus of not having a bunch of hot chicks in it. Not that the chicks in James Bond movies ever get naked anyway. Sometimes James Bond can be so fucking weak. As for this movie, it's *supposed* to be a comedy but the jokes are strictly your lowest-common-denominator shit, like having a long, clumsy title or giving everyone "funny" names like "Jack D. Ripper" and "Colonel Bat Guano." Moviemakers, when are you going to learn that there's nothing less funny in a movie than a funny name? Keep funny names on the playground, where they belong:

"Jenny Keyes, Jenny Keyes, only twelve and on her knees!"

Okay, I guess that's more of a chant than a funny name, but you see what mean. To be fair, there are *some* funny jokes in this flick ("Probably bought them from the Army as war surplus."), but the problem is that there just aren't enough of them. Have you ever seen the movie *Super Troopers* (2001)? If so, you probably noticed that every joke in *Super Troopers* is fucking hysterical, but there's only six of them. The rest of the movie is just filler. *Dr. Strangelove* is a lot like that, except instead of having no jokes at all between the funny ones, this movie has lots of unfunny jokes between the funny ones. If you're one of those people who has to go to the bathroom a lot and can time it right, this might work for you, but for the rest of us waiting for the good parts gets pretty tedious.

You know, old people generally go to the bathroom a lot, don't they? And at this point, only old people really remember or care about the Cold War. I guess that clinches it. This one is recommended for old people only.

Suggested Alternative: *Gas! Or: It Became Necessary to Destroy the World in Order to Save It* (1970)

```
□□□□□□□
```

#35

```
□□□□□□□
```

The Maltese Falcon

(1941)

Drama

This flick takes place in *San Francisco?* I'm sorry, but that was a serious miscalculation. This is a tough-guy detective movie, and tough-guy detective movies really need to go down someplace equally tough, like New York or Chicago or Personville. How hard is it to be tough when everyone around you is a gay hippie?[15]

The story begins when this broad shows up and hires the main guy to find her sister, who's been running around town with some shady creep. From the sound of it the sister is underage, easy, and kinda stupid, so the main guy's partner horns in and jumps all over this one. Seems that wasn't such a hot idea though, because the next thing he knows he's got a bullet in the bloodbox.

As it turns out, the whole "missing sister" story was a ruse. What's really going down is that everybody and their brother's

---

15 Speaking of hippies, this flick actually kicks off with the main guy rolling a joint in his office! I guess that's why they called him "Bogart."

uncle is after this statue of a bird. I forget what kind of bird, but really, it's not important, and neither is the plot frankly because after an hour of scheming and scamming and skullduggery between the four or five bad guys we've already met, a cat we never even saw before just strolls into the main guy's office and the damn bird falls out of his ass. Hell, the movie could've *started out* like that. Seriously, who the fuck was that guy? Oh, my bad - apparently he was "Captain Jacoby, master of the *La Paloma*." As if that's any excuse.

As you can see, this flick might as well not even have a story, but that said there is plenty of badassery, 1940's style. The main guy is especially awesome: he's so ruthless that when his partner gets killed his first priority is changing the name on all their company stationary! Later he orders his client to give him all her money, and when she asks for a little back to live on he tells her that if she needs spending money then she can hock some of her belongings. Same argument I used to use on my second wife.

The main chick is nowhere near as cool though. For one thing, she's way too mediocre to get away her flirty little "Oh please, you *must* help me!" act. It's not like it works on the main guy anyway, but if I was in his gumshoes I'd pop her in the mouth just for peddling that shit without the proper equipment. Now if she looked like, say, Ellie Kemper, or Kimber Riddle, that would be a different story. I'm gonna drop Ke$ha's name here, too. Ke$ha could definitely pull it off.

Unfortunately, the wrap-up is pretty lame. At one point during the "thrilling climax" everyone is just sitting around reading! And what is all this "maybe you love me and maybe I love you" baloney the main guy feeds the main chick at the very end? They've known each other for what, four days? Hell, if you added up all the time they were actually in the same room together it was probably less than twelve hours, and five of those were spent with three other dudes. Don't get me wrong, I believe in love at first sight (especially if it'll get me into someone's pants), but this is just ridiculous.

Suggested Alternative: *The Big Sleep* (1946)

#34

City Lights

(1931)
Comedy

This movie stars Charlie Chaplin, AKA the Little Tramp. (Coincidentally, that was my third wife's nickname too.) You know this guy, even if you think you don't - he sports the bowler hat and the cane and the Hitler mustache, and for years annoying, middle-aged ladies who thought they were being clever would dress up as him for Halloween. For some examples of this, watch every episode of *I Love Lucy* (1951-1957) and *Hart to Hart* (1979-1984) until you find the ones where this happens. Or better yet, don't.

The story, what there is of it, concerns this suicidal rummy who's Charlie Chaplin's best friend when he's loaded but then forgets who he is when he sobers up. This inevitably leads to antics, the vast majority of which would likely be considered zany: people fall on their asses, people fall into the water over and over again, someone pours booze down the front of someone else's pants, there's mistaken identity, a dame's ass is set on fire, someone gets sprayed with a seltzer bottle, a flower pot falls on the main guy's head, and, of course, there's a joke about horse shit. (The main guy just has to clean it up, but this flick is so lowbrow I'm surprised they didn't concoct a scenario where he accidentally eats it or something.) Honestly, how they forgot to include someone farting is beyond me.

Even without any farting it's all simpleton-level humorosity, but I will admit, I did like the drunk driving gag:

Charlie Chaplin: "Be careful how you're driving."
Drunk: "Am I driving?"

Ha ha! Screech all you want, MADD, it's fucking funny.

When the main guy isn't falling down he's chasing after this blind girl (good choice - blind girls are nowhere near as picky as the rest of you bitches), but even though they try to wring some cheapjack sentiment out of this it's painfully obvious that she's only in this movie so they can work in some blind jokes. That's pretty ruthless, but since they already went there, you know what would've been a great gag? The blind chick is driving a car, swerving all over the road and shit, and finally she crashes, at which point Charlie Chaplin, who's riding shotgun, says "I should've known better than to let you drive when you're this drunk!" Now that's fucking comedy.

Suggested Alternative: *Caddyshack* (1980)

Extra Credit Project: Here's something to look for if you ever get stuck watching this flick. Towards the end there's a big boxing match that's in the movie solely to give Charlie Chaplin more excuses to fall down. Big surprise, right? Anyway, between rounds, right about the time when Charlie is imagining that his girl is there, look really closely at the spectators in the background. One of them isn't a person, it's actually an especially creepy-looking mannequin! It's so bizarre and freaky once you notice it. Seriously, *City Lights*, what the fuck?

#33

Chinatown

(1974)
Drama

Hey, it's the main chick from *Bonnie and Clyde* again, already looking kinda used up. I guess the intervening seven years have really *Dunaway* with her youthful good looks! Ha ha ha ha! Oh, and the chick she plays this time around isn't too bright, either:

MAIN GUY: "I was trying to keep someone from being hurt. I ended up making sure that she was hurt."
BONNIE & CLYDE CHICK: "Was there a woman involved?"

What part of "she" is completely over this bimbo's head? Unless she thought he was talking about a boat, or assumed he was doing some politically-correct over-compensating (PCOC) and substituting *she* for the generic *he*. You know, like insecure people do.

At any rate, the story plays out just like one of those old-timey detective movies, except in 1974 they didn't have to worry about the Hayes Code or the Comics Code or Tipper Gore's endless, frigid braying or any of that shit so they were able to include all the things those old movies had to leave out, like blood, tits, and being in color. Also, just for good measure, they throw in a plethora of ho-smackin' and a little incest.[16] In short, it's good shit.

The only real problem with this flick is the main guy. It's the same cat who played the main guy in *The Shining* (1980), and if you know his work then you know that he only has one setting: crazy. That's terrific when he's playing the Joker or a drunk who's been possessed by ghosts and is trying to murder Olive Oyl with an axe, but it gives everything else he plays this weird fucking vibe where no matter how inappropriate it would be to the material you're still kind of waiting for him to snap. Hell, even if he was doing one of the voices in a Disney cartoon you'd still walk out vaguely disappointed when it didn't deteriorate into a total bloodbath. Actually I feel that way about most Disney movies anyway, and I'm sure I'm not the only one. Who wouldn't want to see the Little Mermaid lose the seashell top and come out shooting?

Suggested Alternative: *The Big Lebowski* (1998)

---

16 You have no idea how long I've been looking for an excuse to use the phrase "a plethora of ho-smackin'" in a completely legitimate context. Now if I can just get Laura Silverman and Natasha Leggero to kiss, my bucket list will be complete.

#32

Psycho

(1960)
Horror

In this age of stealing most movies from the Internet and occasionally Best Buy while the sales guy is distracted by my girl's tits,[17] it's hard to imagine what a phenomenon *Psycho* really was when it first came out. This is especially true because for all intents and purposes it was still the 1950's, and trust me when I tell you that movies about cross-dressing serial killers didn't exactly fly back then.

Somehow *Psycho* became this huge thing though, so huge, in fact, that eventually they made three more Psycho movies, all of which, amazingly enough, were pretty good. (Although the twist at the end of Part 2 did set a new record for retarded). There's also a fifth one that nobody likes to talk about called *Bates Motel* (1987), but even that one is fairly decent until the halfway point, when it inexplicably stops being about its own story. Tons of bands have written songs based on *Psycho* too, the two best examples being "Bates Motel" by the Hitmen and "Norman Bates" by Landscape. Huh? The Misfits? Never heard

---

17 Seriously, they're incredible.

of 'em.

With all that in mind it's too bad that there's no real reason for anyone to ever watch this movie again. Why? Because even if you live alone in the Outback and have never had contact with civilization in your entire life you know that the main guy turns out to be a deranged, cross-dressing transvestite who thinks he's his own mom, and that he stabs the main chick to death in the shower. The fact that they actually came out with a remake of this movie in the 1990's, somehow thinking that everyone would be surprised by those parts all over again, finally proved beyond any shadow of a doubt that every single human being who works in Hollywood is goddamned retard. Except of course Alan Spencer. He rocks.

That said, sometimes the journey is the reward, or at least that's what old people always tell me. Frankly this is probably because their journey ended in an old folks' home, and looking back they really wish that they'd taken a few chances in life or at the very least done more drugs. They could be right though, so let's see if there's anything cool in this movie that isn't so goddamned famous that we instinctively know it *in utero*.

So, you can pretty much ignore everything that happens for the first 45 minutes, where the main chick swipes 40 grand from her boss and incompetently flees, because we know she's gonna get croaked so literally none of it matters. (It is kind of amusing how hilariously dumb this trick is though. If she didn't get murdered by *someone* she was bound to fall into a hole or accidentally drink poison sooner or later anyway.) Next there's the big scene where she gets murdered in the shower,[18] and then we have to watch the main guy clean up the place, which, needless to say is pretty boring.

Okay, so now we're an hour in...

Eventually a private dick (heh) comes snooping around and *he* gets stabbed (this part's not bad), and later the dead chick's sister and boyfriend turn up and find a *way* too how-fucking-convenient clue in the toilet:

SISTER: "It didn't get washed down. Look. Some figure has been added to or subtracted from 40,000. That proves Marion was here."

Yes, only Marion could be involved with something that totals 40,000. That bitch fucking *owns* the number 40,000. It would've been a lot more accurate if the piece of paper they found just said "Duh."

I'm sorry, but all told once you get past the cross-dressing and the shower murder there's not that much going on here. The "thrilling" climax isn't even a chase or a big fight or anything, it's just a bunch of yelling. I don't know about you, but I can't stand it when people are yelling and screaming all the time. It gets on my damn nerves.

Suggested Alternative: *Halloween* (1978)

---

18 This is a Titless Shower Scene™, by the way, and seeing as it's the most famous shower scene of all time, it set a pretty shitty precedent.

#31

The Gold Rush

(1925)

Comedy

Oh no, not Charlie Chaplin *again*. For real, movie critics, falling down just isn't that funny. This time the Little Whore is supposedly prospecting for gold, but don't be fooled: his real agenda is to steal as much shit as humanly possible. Food, shots, even a house *Beverly Hills Cop II* style, he swipes it all. Oh, and he utterly trashes another guy's pad, for absolutely no reason, after he's asked to house-sit. What an asshole.

Of course the jokes are all low-brow, slapstick idiocy from before the dawn of time, to the point where they even pull out the old "we're so hungry we're going to eat a shoe" bit, and the "I'm so hungry another person looks like a big chicken" deal. Okay, fine, this movie's pretty fossilized so maybe they invented those gags, but that doesn't make them any less lame. Oh, and I really hate to nit-pick, but there's a dog in one part that keeps looking at the camera! You're breaking the fourth wall, you stupid fucking dog! If you wanna make it in this business at least know the basics. Don't make us chop you up for horse food.

Factual Fact: One easy way to identify someone as a fag is if they refer to Charlie Chaplin, or anyone else for that matter, as a "silent clown." For real, it's physically impossibly to say those two words, in that order, if you've never had a penis in your mouth. Go ahead and try it right now.

Suggested Alternative: *Goldfinger* (1964)

#30

Amadeus

(1984)
Drama

I cannot believe that song by Falco isn't in this movie. You know the one I mean - "Der Kommisar."

That aside, having the main guy's sworn enemy tell the story is kind of a cool angle, sort of like having Lex Luthor narrate *Superman VIII*, but there's no getting past the fact that this is a super long movie about classical music, and classical music is generally pretty boring unless helicopters are attacking people to it or you're boning some hottie from behind while singing *The Barber of Seville*. Because let's face it, that would be hilarious.

This movie is all lush and historical too, two more things people hate, and, worst of all, Amadeus himself is pretty fucking obnoxious and spending this much time with him when he's not picking up the bar tab is pretty intolerable. You might think it's unlikely that a movie would make its main guy that annoying, but trust me, the first time you hear Amadeus cackle you'll want him deader than that kid with the patchy mustache who knocked up your daughter.

This movie doesn't disappoint in that regard at least: Amadeus does die, although it takes three fucking hours for this to finally happen. And after all of his trials and tribulations (not to mention ours – three goddamned hours, remember?) his only two legacies are 1) reams of music that most people find even more boring than U2 and 2) this movie, which makes him look like he was an unbearably irritating asshole. I'm sure he appreciates *that*.

Still, as far as movies about classical music guys go this is infinitely better than the one about Richard Wagner (which is basically just five hours of Wagner moving his piano from place to place), and if nothing else the chick playing Mrs. Amadeus is super fine and we actually get to see her tits. I'll sing *The Barber of Seville* to that one any day.

By the way, I found out where that kid with the patchy mustache lives. Call me.

Suggested Alternative: *Marie Antoinette* (2006)

■■■■■■■■

#29

■■■■■■■■

Midnight Cowboy

(1969)

Drama

This flick got famous the easy way, by being rated X. The twist? It isn't porn.[19] Naturally it was the thing to see in 1969, but watching it this long after the fact is like making a movie based on *The Simpsons* (1989-the end of time) ten years after anyone still cared. Of course they did that too, so here we are.

As the movie begins, this dork is dressing himself up like the kind of cowboy who fucks other cowboys, for money, on stage, in Soho, while crying. Then he catches a bus to New York City, where he thinks he's gonna become a male prostitute. I see a lot of poorly-sucked cocks in *his* future. Once he gets to New York he's immediately bamboozled this guy who's *walkin' here,* but latter they become pals and have various adventures, including a scene where they go around town stealing everything from laundry to a shoe shine and a scene where

---

19 Of course, plenty of horror movies from the 1970's can make this claim too, but none of them had a chance of making this list because most movie critics live in a magical fantasy world where horror movies don't exist and all those teenagers and black people they saw lined up at the AMC were really there to see some French flick.

they attend a party that's weird just for the sake of being weird, which I found particularly tiresome because believe me, once you've seen a few movie parties like this they're not so much weird as straight-up annoying. Oh, and along the way some gay dick is indeed sucked. Remember when I called it? I totally called it. These two clowns do have a long-term plan though. They want to go to Florida, mainly because the *I'm walking here* guy thinks that everything will be better if he can just make it to Florida. Lots of people from the north feel this way, so let me give you all a piece of advice: when you get to Florida, you're still going to be you. Living near the beach doesn't cure being a perpetual fuck-up.

Of course it all ends in tragedy, specifically when I'm Walking Here dies on the bus to Miami. What makes this part stupid is that it's one of those scenes where someone is just blathering on and on and doesn't even realize that the person they're talking to is dead until they don't answer. You see this bit in movies all the time and it pisses me off because it's totally unrealistic. Everybody knows that you immediately shit and piss yourself when you die, which means that this scene really should've played out more like this:

MAIN GUY: "I got this damn thing all figured out. When we get to Miami, what I'm gonna do is..."
OTHER GUY: [Sound of the loudest, foulest, nastiest death shit imaginable.]
MAIN GUY: "Hey! I just bought you those pants!"

Suggested Alternative: *Drugstore Cowboy* (1989)

#28

The African Queen

(1951)
Adventure

There's nothing more important to fat, white people than forcing everyone else to believe in Jesus. Okay, maybe deep-fried cheese, but that's it. The fat, white guy in this movie pays for it though when the Nazis bust up his little African church (the First Methodist Church of Kung Fu) and burn the local village to the ground. And with no... what do you call it?... indignant culture left for him to destroy he gets so depressed that he dies.

So as you can see, at least some good has come of all this.

Unfortunately, his frigid, bitchy, hag sister is still sucking air. She hitches a ride on this one guy's boat, and then convinces him, primarily through nagging, that he should sail through some dangerous rapids and then blow himself up in an insane suicide mission so that she can get back to England that much sooner to have her fucking tea. Why he puts up with this obnoxious twat for more than five seconds is a complete mystery (she's not worth screwing, and no one would ever miss her if he just threw her over the side), but it might have something to do with the fact that *he's the biggest fucking pussy I have ever seen in my entire life.* He doesn't even do anything when the raging cunt dumps two entire *cases* of gin overboard! Except whine like a bitch, of course. I've seen baby girls who just lost their favorite dolly man up more than this faggot.

One thing I hadn't seen before though is anything as creepy (or nauseating) as the moments when they make it clear that the main guy does, in fact, want this old bag's dried-up mummy pussy. I'm not too proud to admit that I puked when the two of them finally got it on. Thank god this movie was made back in uptight days and they couldn't actually show it.

As for the adventure we signed on for, it's all so fucking lame that the process should be copyrighted. It's just a bunch of fill-in-the-blanks shit like guys with bad aim shooting at them, some rapids, and the old accidentally going over a waterfall bit. How do people in adventure movies manage to accidentally go over so many waterfalls anyway? Aren't things like that generally marked on maps? The part where the main guy is teasing these hippos held *some* promise (it's a little-known fact, but hippos are actually pretty dangerous and kill more people each year than sharks, lawn darts, and kids bringing toy army men to school combined), but ultimately the hippos don't attack them so that scene was a bust too.

In the end the Nazis catch these two clowns and decide to hang them as spies, but as a final request they ask the kraut in charge to marry them first. To each other, I mean. This leads to the only good line in the entire movie:

NAZI CAPTAIN: "By the authority invested in me by Kaiser Wilhelm the Second I pronounce you man and wife. Proceed with the execution."

Ha! In an honest world, they would say that at every wedding. Now, in a truly kickass adventure movie the very next scene would be the Nazis throwing the hag to the crocodiles, who would eat her as slowly as possible. This would also take care of the main guy, because I'm sure he would cry himself to death over it. That's not what happens though. Instead, an unbelievably well-timed contrivance drops right out of someone's ass, the main guy and the hag are saved at the last possible minute, and they both live happily ever after. The end.

What a bunch of weak-ass bullshit. This movie couldn't be more pussified if it had a tampon *and* my dick in it.

Suggested Alternative: *Fitzcarraldo* (1982)

░░░░░░░

#27

░░░░░░░

It Happened One Night

(1934)
Comedy

With some movies and TV shows, the whole premise is so beyond stupid that you can't even begin to take it seriously. Take *Prison Break* (2005-2009) for example. *Prison Break* was about a guy whose brother is in jail for – what else? – a crime he didn't commit. So does he hire a really good lawyer to file an appeal, or drive through the prison wall with a tank? Nope, he has the prison blueprints tattooed onto his body, gets himself arrested, and lands in the very same prison, where he uses the tattoo to bust his brother out from the inside. It's textbook retarded, and will undoubtedly be remembered for decades if not centuries to come as the single stupidest fucking setup for a TV show in the history of the world.

Then there's this piece of crap. The main chick in this movie gets kidnapped, held prisoner on a yacht, and even slapped around a little bit, but when she finally escapes every cop in the country is on the case so they can *return her to the kidnappers*. Okay, so the cat who kidnapped her is all Daddy Warbucks and shit, but do they really expect us to believe that *every single cop in the United States* is crooked and this one guy has ALL of them on his payroll? Frankly I'd like to punch the pinhead who wrote this flick in the stomach just for insulting my intelligence. And I think I'd do it after he ate a huge meal too, so he'd puke all over the place in front of everybody. With any luck he'd be so embarrassed that he'd start crying, too. That would be awesome.

So anyway, our main chick is on the run, and she ends up hooking up with this drunk reporter who helps her out so he can get the scoop. Along the way they have all these weird, clunky conversations that I guess are somebody's idea of cute, or clever, or something, and after a while the movie just tosses the original plot out the window entirely so it can concentrate on these two falling in love. Oh, you were actually kind of interested in how that original plot was going to play out, you say? Too bad.

I'm sure you can guess what happens next. That's right, there's a series of misunderstandings of the type that only occur in stupid romantic comedies where everyone acts like a complete fucking moron, and as a result the chick runs off to marry this other douche instead, even though he apparently has certain... inadequacies. And it's not like she doesn't know it: "Promise you'll never let me get off," she says. If you further guessed that it all gets straightened at the last possible second and the main chick and the reporter get back together and live happily ever after, then congratulations. Here's your Oscar©®™© for sucking.

Suggested Alternative: *Something Wild* (1986)

#26

High Noon

(1952)
Western

I'll tell ya, I have had plenty of these in my day. Sometimes it just can't wait until 4:20, am I right?

Welp, the sheriff has just turned in his resignation so he can get down to business, and business is fucking his new wife. But then these crooks pick that exact moment to ride into town and let it be known that a cat's arriving on the noon train to shoot the sheriff's face off. The ultimate cock-block.

Of course the sheriff could just vamoose before said cat arrives, but you know how guys are - he starts strutting around and talking about how he can't do that for some vague reason that he never quite lays out but we all know involves the perceived size of his penis. The sheriff does try to round up a posse to back him up, but no one else wants to get involved in this little pissing match - not the deputy, not the Christians, not the obnoxious Mexican twat, not even the Wolf Man. In fact, the only people willing to pick up a shootin' iron and help out are a kid and a dude who's only got one eye. This isn't a slapstick comedy though, so the sheriff tells them to git.

So now we wait and wait and wait and wait and wait while nothing happens. To the people who made this movie, standing in line at the Bureau of Motor Vehicles must qualify as "nail-biting suspense." I'm not kidding, except for one brawl it's just endless hanging around until the very end when the noon train *finally* shows up.

Now, if I was in charge of making this movie I would've pulled some hilarious, infuriating twist at this point that punked everybody, like having it turn out that the bad guy isn't even on the train because he missed his connection in Albuquerque. He's on board though, and there is a showdown, but believe me when I tell you that it definitely isn't worth the wait. And why the fuck does one of the bad guys bust out a store window and steal a ladies' hat on his way to the big gunfight? Is he planning on doing a little cross-dressing afterwards? "Can't you wait?" says his buddy. "Just wanna be ready," he explains. For real, dude, there's a time and a place for everything. What the hell's the matter with you?

Suggested Alternative: *The Quick and the Dead* (1995)

#25

Some Like It Hot

(1959)
Comedy

Apparently some like it gay, too. Seriously, this is the second cross-dressing movie on this list, leading me to believe that all mainstream movie critics are secretly raging queers. Ha! I'm kidding of course. There's nothing secret about it.

This flick does start off with some cool Prohibition shenanigans,[20] but the featured hilarity actually begins with a brutal slaying. Two guys see the murder go down and now the killers are after them, so they immediately go to the police for protection and to tell them what they know. Oh, wait, my bad, that wouldn't be zany (or stupid) enough. Instead, they disguise themselves as chicks and join this all-bim band that's heading down to Florida for a three-week gig.

Now, like in most movies where dudes dress up as chicks, it's super-obvious that they're men and even a blind person

---

20 For those of you who failed History and were forced to repeat it, Prohibition was this terrible time when a bunch of chicks talked everyone into making booze completely illegal. They agreed to have the law repealed though when all the ugly ones stopped getting laid.

186

wouldn't be fooled for a second. But naturally everyone in this flick is. And *of course* there's some clueless guy who thinks that one of the dudes in drag is the hottest thing he's ever seen and just won't take no for an answer, because it isn't enough that this awful fucking bit wasn't funny the other 8000 times we've seen it. (Actually, there's at least *two* guys in this flick who think that one of the dudes in drag is the hottest thing on wheels and won't take no for an answer. Writing is hard.) As you can imagine the story is made up almost entirely of insultingly juvenile slapstick antics, but the absolute worst kick in the dick is at the end, where the very gangsters who are after the two main guys just *happen* to show up for a crooks convention at the very hotel where said main guys are hiding out. How fucking convenient.

Some may indeed like it hot. Me, I like it not an insult to my intelligence.

Suggested Alternative: *Sometimes Aunt Martha Does Dreadful Things* (1971)

#24

The Godfather Part II

(1974)
Drama

Jesus dago-whacking Christ, aren't there any *short* mob movies? If the real mob was anything like the movies they'd never do any crimes because it would take them a decade just to decide who to rob. Maybe if they didn't kick this damn flick off with half an hour of *meetings* they would've been in a better mindset to rein it in a bit. I mean really, if I wanted to spend half an hour in a meeting, I'd actually show up at the office once in a while. Things do pick up eventually, but frankly all the Godfather movies are too concerned with being pretentious and not concerned enough with being utterly badass. If nothing else though, they are a gentle reminder of a simpler time, when the stereotype was that all Eye-talians were in the mob. Now that the stereotype is an orange midget who looks like a pot-bellied pig that's been trained to walk on its hind legs and suck cock, most Italians probably long for those days.

Total Wop Kills: 14

Suggested Alternative: *Scarface* (1983)

■■■■■■■■

#23

■■■■■■■■

It's a Wonderful Life

(1946)

Drama

This used to be one of those movies that was in the "public domain." This meant that no one company legally owned it and it belonged to the world, which is not too dissimilar to how my third wife felt about her pussy. When something is in the public domain any TV station can run it as often as they want and it doesn't cost them one thin dime, so for years, around Christmastime, this movie was on television so fucking much that before long there wasn't a single person on Earth who didn't hate the shit out of it.[21] It got so bad that finally someone hired a dickload of lawyers and actually found a way to buy the thing, just to keep people from showing it any more.

So, as a kid the main guy in this movie has a pretty admirable dream - when he grows up, he wants a harem! Things don't work out the way he planned though. First, he gets sucked into

---

21 Why Christmastime? Because the story goes down on Christmas, and apparently that was enough for most people to declare it a Christmas movie, despite the fact that Christmas itself doesn't even play into the story. I mean really, *Die Hard* (1988) goes down on Christmas, and no one considers that a goddamned Christmas movie.

running his dad's building & loan, which gives out all these high-risk loans to people with little or no collateral (thanks a lot, dick). At some point his brother is supposed to take over the business so our main guy can finally get to work on that harem, but then the brother shows up with his new wife (who, for some reason, is sporting a hat made out of paper plates and chopsticks) and naturally they've got plans of their own, so the main guy eats it again. And again. And again.

Basically, he spends the next several years stuck in his pissant, white bread hometown watching all his dreams go up in smoke, until finally he can't stand it anymore and decides to kill himself. Now, in a lot of movies this is when the miracle would occur, but as far as divine intervention goes this one's leaning a lot more towards Job than it is towards, uh, I dunno, some Bible story where God was nice. See, instead of fixing the main guy's circumstances, God sends an angel to convince him to accept his crappy life as-is. How does the angel do this? By showing him how much worse his hometown would be if he had never been born. And what's one of the very first things we see in this "bad" version of town? A black person! Ha ha ha ha ha ha ha! You can't tell me they didn't do that on purpose.

Racism aside, ultimately this movie is about giving up on your dreams, being forced to settle, and a callous, spiteful god who won't even let you escape into the sweet embrace of death. It's a wonderful life!

Suggested Alternative: Killing yourself

#22

Treasure of the Sierra Madre

(1948)

Adventure

This dude is stranded in Tampico (you know, where they make that nasty-ass fruit drink), so he finds himself a job in order to earn enough bread to ship out. The guy who hired him rips him off though, so he teams up with another joker the guy conned and the two of them track the prick down, at which point they get into the clumsiest bar fight in movie history (translation: the most realistic). Even after they roll that fool their finances ain't so hot, so they hook up with this third cat who says that there's gold in them thar hills.

Now, I'd always assumed that this was a big adventure movie, like Indiana Jones or something, but as it turns out nearly the entire story is about these three clowns prostrating for gold and then arguing with each other when they actually find some. I'll tell you one thing, after they hit the mother load there is plenty of gold to go around, and if I was in their shoes I wouldn't be all paranoid and distrustful and accusatory, constantly scheming and scamming and looking over my shoulder for weeks on end. No way. I'd shoot every single one of my partners immediately and be done with it. In fact, I'd cook and eat 'em too, or at least violate their corpses. Hey, if you're gonna be evil, you might as well go all the way.

So anyhow, these Frito banditos eventually show up, and after one of them says "We don't need no stinkin' badges!" so that hack comedy writers will have a completely out-of-context line to riff on for centuries to come, they steal all the main guys' shit: burros, gold, supplies, credit cards, the whole shebang. Get this though - instead of keeping the gold, the bandits dump it all on the ground and then try to sell the *burros* for money! Jesus claim-jumping Christ, is this movie trying to say that Mexicans are so fucking stupid that they don't even know what gold is? Is that seriously what this fucking retarded movie is trying to tell us? If I was some taco-swilling wetback spic I'd be highly offended. Hell, I'm offended anyway. I know that every single time people in a movie find some fabulous treasure the story just *has* to end with them losing it ironically because that's so clever and original, but this, this is a total insult to my intelligence. Fuck this piece of shit.

Suggested Alternative: *Treasure of the Four Crowns* (1983)

#21

Vertigo

(1958)
Thriller

You know that effect where it looks like something is coming towards you and the background is moving away from you at the same time? That was invented for this movie. Of course nowadays they use that effect to depict everything from being frightened by a ghost to finding out that there's no more beer in the fridge, but originally it was meant to show that the main guy in this flick has *acrophobia,* which is officially defined as the fear off falling off shit.[22] It's an especially bad condition to have in a movie, because, as you may have noticed, whenever someone in a movie is being chased, they always want to climb something, and the higher and more dangerous, the better. People in movies are generally pretty stupid.

It starts out like a horror movie. This dude asks the main guy to follow his wife, acrophobia or no, because he thinks she's possessed by a ghost. She was probably just PMSing, but the

---

22 "Acrophobia" is a terrible name for a movie though, so they went with *Vertigo.* That's misleading however. Vertigo is actually caused by drinking too many rum sours.

dude is an old pal so the main guy agrees to do it. Whatever the bitch's problem is, eventually she's so far gone that she tries to kill herself, so the main guy has no choice - he starts boning her. What a douchebag. Still, he is a lot more motivated to solve the mystery now, so when the wife has a strange dream about this Spanish mission he takes her there. Where she immediately jumps out of a tower and dies. Oops! Ha ha!

Needless to say the main guy's feeling pretty guilty now, or maybe just horny, but either way he starts hanging around all the places the wife used to go. That's right, he's stalking a *dead chick*. Our hero, ladies and gentlemen. Then, one day, he sees this broad who looks just like dead girl, so he starts stalking *her* and somehow, by being as creepy as possible, he convinces her to have dinner with him.

Ah, but there's a reason she didn't just blast him with pepper spray immediately: it seems that everything that happened previously was, in fact, a huge scam! As it turns out, the buddy set up this whole rigamarole so he could kill his wife - she's the one who took the tumble, and the chick the main dude's in love with was just the ringer. Frankly the whole thing seems needlessly complicated, and the part where the second girl somehow manages to fall out of the exact same tower as the wife is like poetic justice for retards, but when the dust clears the main guy's vertigo is vertigo-go-gone so I guess he came out okay at least. Oh, and they never do mention the husband again, so I guess he got away with it. Everybody wins.

Suggested Alternative: *High Anxiety* (1977)

#20

The Graduate

(1967)
Comedy

Hey, I totally get it - finally graduating from college sucks. That's why you shouldn't do it. Me, I changed my major 37 times before I got my first degree, and even then it was kind of an accident. I never should've entered that rafting race.

Ultimately this movie isn't really about that though. What's it's really about is a guy who's trying to pull off the old mother-daughter combo. For those of you who are super sheltered (i.e. Christians), that's when you manage to nail a chick *and* her daughter.[23] Along the way the main guy is forced to wear scuba gear at a party, gets all nervous about boning the mom, acts like a jerk on purpose to ruin this date he's forced to go on (bad move - that's the surest way to get a girl to fall for you, which of course is exactly what happens), and so on and so forth.

As you can see, this movie has all the necessary ingredients for a zany teen sex comedy, but the twist is that instead of making

23 It doesn't have to be at the same time, although that would be pretty boss. Also, it doesn't count if the daughter is also *your* daughter.

it funny, they made it pretentious. That's right - this is a madcap sex comedy without the comedy. And, truth be told, it could use a lot more sex too. It's also one of those moronic movies that expects us to buy it when two people fall in love after a single date. Okay, really, come the fuck on. I was married to my first wife for twelve years and still wasn't in love with her. And she had way bigger tits than the chick in this movie, let me tell you.

Since they dispensed with the humorousity I assume we're supposed to take this movie semi-seriously, but how is that even possible when you're dealing with such dreamy, flakey idiots? They probably fall in love every time they get a haircut, or fall off a boat. Who cares if doesn't work out this time? They're sure to meet someone special outside of Target or in the drive-thru at Taco Den before too long.

Suggested Alternative: *The Last American Virgin* (1982)

■■■■■■■

#19

■■■■■■■

West Side Story

(1961)
Musical

This movie is about gangs, but in much the same way that *Half Baked* (1998) is about drug addiction, or *Hannah Montana* is about the rock & roll lifestyle. Seriously, if it was the prancing silver faggots of *West Side Story* vs. say, the Hugga Bunch, my money would be on the Hugga Bunch. And frankly, I can't even remember exactly what they were. I think little teddy bears, right?

There's basically two gangs. We'll call one the "Snapper Carrs" because they snap their fingers all the time, and we'll call the other one the "Hispanic Homos" because their c-c-c-colors are mulberry and mauve. Now, they are constantly throwing down, but their "rumbles" are a combination of goofy slapstick and blatant gay flirting, and even their graffiti is laughable beyond belief. One particularly vicious dis tag, for example, says that the other gang "stinks." Hey, now. Kids might be watching.

The actual story begins when the main guy – who used to run (and dance! and sing!) with the Snapper Carrs – suffers a sudden bout of shared glaucoma with this chick at a dance, and unless you also have glaucoma I think you'll see where this is going. That's right, her brother's a Hispanic Homo, and it's fucking *Romeo and Juliet* (1594) all over again. These fools are on the fast track to tragedy too, because they fall in love even quicker than the dipshits from *The Graduate*. Here's what the guy sings like an hour after he meets this trick:

"And there's nothing for me but Maria
Every sight that I see is Maria
I'll commit sodomy with Maria..."

I may not have transcribed that exactly, but you get the point. She gets it too:

Maria: "When you come, use the back door."

Things do pick up somewhat towards the end – a few people actually die, and before someone stops them I swear the Carrs were just about to shove one of their own head-first right up this Puerto Rican chick's pussy – but frankly it's all too little too late. And this movie doesn't even pass muster as a very special cautionary example, because truth be told it mostly makes gangbanging look like it's goofy, colorful, and fun. The next time you read about a 5-year-old who was riddled with stray bullets during a drive-by, I think you can safely blame *West Side Story*.

Suggested Alternative: *The Warriors* (1979)

[film strip graphic]

#18

[film strip graphic]

The Wizard of Oz
(1939)
Musical

You know, I tried that thing once where you sync this flick up with a Pink Floyd record, and I gotta say, it was the most depressing 43 minutes of my life. No wonder that munchkin hanged himself. In hindsight though, maybe I should've used the album they suggested instead of *The Final Cut.*

Okay, a lot of people don't know this, but there are literally millions of Oz movies. This is just the most famous. In fact, on my website (www.mrsatanism.com) I once reviewed one Oz movie a day, every day, for a month. (Excluding weekends. That's when I drink.) I could never figure out why the main actress in this one is such a huge gay icon though. Don't gay dudes, by definition, prefer other dudes? I've actually asked a few gay dudes about this, but the ones I talked to didn't know because they were all under 50 and their gay icon was the guy from Erasure.

Irregardless, I'm a straight guy and I'd love to meet Dorothy in real life, especially after seeing how easily Uncle Marvel coerces her into the back of his trailer. "Yeah, baby, Oz is right here, in the back of my van. The windows are blacked out to prevent all the rainbows from escaping." And speaking of Marvel, did you ever notice that he *steals* that picture of Dorothy and her aunt after he looks at it? I guess he needed some new spank material.

Of course Oz itself is home to way bigger creeps than a pervert member of the extended Marvel Family. Sure, there's the evil witch Dorothy pulps with her house and the backup witch who wants to murder her, but I was thinking more of the Lollipop Guild. I mean really, is there anyone on Earth who doesn't utterly despise those obnoxious little bastards? Every time I see this movie I have dreams for weeks afterwards where I'm tying all three of them to a tree, covering them with honey, and then just waiting for the ants. Oh, and while I'm waiting I'm running through the entire 'Sutra with Dorothy, who, just to keep it interesting, is dressed as Alice in Wonderland.

Getting back to the witches, don't think for a minute that I'm letting Glinda – the "good" witch – off the hook. I mean really, does anyone actually buy that crap about Dorothy needing to learn some valuable lesson before the ruby slippers will take her home? Let's face it: Dorothy could've clicked her heels together and gone back to Kansas any time she wanted to. Glinda played her like a fiddle in service of her true agenda - bumping off the Wicked Witch of the West once and for all. It's always easier to cover your tracks if you get someone else to do the wet work, isn't it Glinda? And with both wicked witches dead, I'm sure it wouldn't be long before Glinda consolidated her power, established herself as the ruling head of Oz, and inevitably ran their economy completely into the ground. You know how those "good" witches are. Tax and spend, tax and spend.

Politics and the Lollipop Guild aside though, this is a pretty good movie, although there is one major plot point that they completely forget to resolve: the angry old lady who takes Dorothy's little dog away. We see the dog escape of course, but that lady seemed pretty determined and I don't doubt for a minute that she's eventually coming back to take the little dog again. Unless Dorothy really did kill the bitch during her extended blackout/fugue state.

Suggested Alternative: *Willy Wonka & the Chocolate Factory* (1971) (Sorry, but Veruca Salt is way hotter than Dorothy Gale.)

██████████

#17

██████████

E.T. - The Extra-Terrestrial
(1982)
Sci-Fi

E.T.? E. fucking T.??? Of all Of Steven Spielberg's movies – no, of all of *anybody's* movies – *this* makes the top 20? This smarmy, cutesy, sickening, sugar-coated, candy shell-coated puke-fest? One of the two worst things about being alive in 1982 was that you couldn't go *anywhere* without somehow being exposed to E. motherpricking T.[24] It wouldn't have been so bad if E.T. was cute, or a girl with no clothes on, but, despite what you've been brainwashed into thinking, E.T. is *not* cute. He looks like a cross between a 112-year-old Indian woman (7-11, not casino), *The Manitou* (1978), and beef jerky. There isn't even a fetish for such a hideous monstrosity, and his creepy-ass extendable neck is like some sort of torture-dildo. Admittedly, there probably is a fetish for the neck.

I saw his movie though (it was mandated by law), but even before I knew what E.T looked like I hated him. You know that part at the very beginning where the little turd is running away from those guys in the woods? (Actually it looks more like he's

---

24 The other one? Same sentence, but replace "E.T." with "Eye of the Tiger".

on rollers and some grip making minimum wage is just pulling him along, but irregardless you know the part I mean.) He's all "Eeeeeeeeeeeeeee! Eeeeeeeeeeeeeee!" and I prayed to God they'd catch him and stomp the living shit out of him, just so he'd shut the fuck up already.

Unfortunately he escapes, and before long this idiot kid named "Smelliot" finds him. Now, to a being capable of intergalactic travel, this kid's intellect is probably a step or two above something his people would kill with a topical lotion, but Smelliot still manages to coerce E.T. into his house by laying down a trail of candy. Are you kidding me? The skunk in my basement didn't even fall for that. And why, why, why does E.T. establish an ESP link with Smelliot? Stephen King didn't write this movie, so the only reason I can figure is that E.T. wants to ensure that if someone decides to shoot first and perform the alien autopsy later, the kid dies too. Call it a little insurance policy, puny earthlings.

Later in the story E.T. disappears, and I will admit, the part where Smelliot's brother finally finds him laying in a filthy ditch, looking like an overripe sausage and being gnawed on by a raccoon, makes me cheer every time. Welcome to Earth, motherfucker.

The rest of this flick is like an endless parade of unicorns shitting a thousand chocolate rainbows though. Who could forget, even after therapy, the part where E.T. hides in plain slight amongst some stuffed animals, or the part where the little girl dresses him up, or the part where the bike flies across the moon, or the part where love brings the goddamned little git back to life, or the frigging rainbow trail the spaceship leaves behind at the end... It's all so fucking corny and gay. The truly mind-boggling part though is that Steven Spielberg went back and George Lucased this movie to make it even *more* pussified. I won't watch that version because I have a soul, but rumor has it he took out the line "It was nothing like that, penis breath!" because it might offend people who don't brush their teeth after they suck cock, and supposedly he also used computer effects to remove the FBI agents' guns because, as we all know, FBI agents don't really carry guns. They carry gumdrops for all the good little boys and girls to... *Are we in international waters yet? Good! Shove it up his ass and pull the pin! SHOVE IT UP HIS FILTHY ASS AND PULL THE FUCKING PIN!!!!!!!!!!!!!!!!!!!*

Sorry, had a little flashback there to a federal gig I had once. Anyway, I suppose for the sake of journalistic integrity I should have fast-forwarded through the bastardized edition and confirmed if any of this is true or not, but my source is an anonymous crank on the Internet and that's good enough for me. Besides, I can't spend all day watching *E.T.* I need some time to drink beer and fuck bitches too.

Fun Fact: They almost made a sequel to this movie called "E.T. II: Nocturnal Fears," which would've been about a bunch of *evil* E.T.s alien-abducting people. I must admit, that almost sounds cool, but you know what I'd really like to see? A sequel where we find out how the kids in Part 1 turned out as adults. I mean, after you fly through the air on a bicycle with a friendly space alien, the rest of your life has to be kind of a letdown. I'll bet most of them became heroin addicts.

Suggested Alternative: *Alien* (1979)

#16

Raging Bull

(1980)
Drama

The fact that boxing even exists is hilariously retarded. You can't just go to a sports bar and spill someone's beer if you want to see a fight? You have to pay 200 bucks to watch dudes wearing sissy gloves do it? And that's just on the Pay-Per-View. If you wanna see a boxing match live, you've either already done it, or you can't afford to.

The main guy in this flick is a violent asshole, and that I can live with. My real problem with him is that he's dumb as dirt. For example, he takes *everything* people say 100% literally, which might work in the context of a wacky comedy about a foreigner who comes to America and doesn't fully understand our language so hilarious misunderstandings ensue, but it doesn't exactly fly in a goddamned boxing movie.

Not that this is really much of a boxing movie to begin with. What with all the disagreeable greaseballs creeping around it plays out more like a mob movie, except with scenes of people punching women standing in for the scenes where people would normally be getting whacked. In fact, there's no standard sports movie angles in this flick at all - there's no part where someone has to win a "the big game" or overcome the odds for the Gipper or any of that shit. Hell, this boxing movie is so not about boxing that instead of a boxing match they wrap it all up with the main guy doing stand-up comedy! Oh, and since it has the flavor of a mob movie naturally that midget loudmouth from *Casino* and *Goodfellas* just has to show up and peddle his tiresome, obnoxious shtick. I swear, the actor who plays this guy must have a standing rule that he won't take any role unless the character description includes the words "violent" "irrational" and "annoying beyond belief."

In summary, if you want to watch a boxing movie that's not about boxing and is full of annoying assholes, this is definitely the film for you. Me, I think the title is a perfect description.

Suggested Alternative: *Bunny & the Bull* (2009)

```
■■■■■■■■
```

#15

```
■■■■■■■■
```

The Best Years of Our Lives

(1946)

Drama

Note: You can find my original review of this flick at my website, www.mrsatanism.com, unless the site is gone by the time you read this book because you're way in the future or it's still regular times but I forgot to pay the hosting bill. If that's the case, then too bad for you because it was totally awesome, and I even included some pictures of topless girls. Also, I'm pretty sure one of them was your sister. You might want to ask her about that.

Satan's blade, why is this movie so fucking long? If you wanted to get a job as a clock-watcher, this movie would be good training because believe me you'll spend the entire time watching the clock, begging for it to be over. For real, I could've seen *two* movies in the time it took to get through this one, and if I had I guarantee that at least one of them would've had some tits in it.

The story's about these three military guys who just got home after giving the Nazis and their dirty Jap butt-buddies the business *and* the what-for, and to be fair it starts out okay with everybody getting plastered, but it's not long before the whining begins. Oh, boo-hoo, I can't find a decent job. Oh, boo-hoo, I *can* find a decent job. Oh, boo-hoo, they had to replace my hands with hooks and now everybody stares at me. Christ, you'd think they just got back from Vietnam. I expected way more from World War Part 2 dudes.

Actually I can sort of sympathize with the hooks guy, because I have a physical condition that draws unwanted attention myself - a shockingly large penis. And sure, one hook hand might be pretty convenient for opening cans or doing battle with that boy who never grew up (you know who I mean - he lives at the Y), but *two* hook hands? That's brutal. You couldn't even... well, I already mentioned my penis once in this review so you can probably guess where I'm going with this. No need to spell it out and offend the ladies. *Or thrill them.*

Anyway, a bunch more boring shit happens, including tons of peripheral whining, a guy visiting the drug store where he used to work, another cat going to the bank, Hooks target-shooting in the work shed in preparation for his inevitable killing spree... blah blah blah. Finally they wrap it all up with a wedding, which is thematically appropriate at least since that's how the best years of most people's lives end. Ha ha! Seriously though, never get married.

Suggested Alternative: *First Blood* (1982)

■■■■■■■

#14

■■■■■■■

One Flew Over the Cuckoo's Nest

(1975)

Drama

Okay, at one point the main guy in this flick decides that his fellow nuthouse inmates don't get enough stimulation, so he decides that they should *watch baseball and go fishing,* the two most boring, mind-numbing activities known to man. Outside of watching grass dry or sitting through an entire *CSI: Miami* marathon, of course. I think he's a little unclear on the concept.

Actually, when you stop to think about it a lot of shit that happens in this movie doesn't make any sense, like the part where our main guy goes through all this rigmarole to sneak onto this bus when his entire group was being taken onto the bus anyway. (I understand that he wants to steal the bus, but the keys are already in it! All he would've had to do was walk on board with everyone else, plop down in the driver's seat, and take off.) Or hell, what about the entire premise, which has this same main guy bending over backwards to stick up for a bunch of crazies only to find out that they're all in the nuthouse voluntarily and can leave any time they want? Not one of these assholes thought to tell him this before? They should've at least filled him in before he got the people in charge so pissed off that they gave him shock therapy. After the shock therapy incident the main guy decides that he's busting out, and his escape attempt is going great until he gets drunk and passes out right in the middle of it! Not long after the folks in charge give him a lobotomy, which was only shocking to me because by this point I was convinced that he didn't have a brain at all.

Let's recap: this is a story about a guy who raises hell in service to nobody, takes a nap instead of escaping when he has the chance, and then ends up a vegetable, all due solely to his own raging stupidity. What a complete fucking tool. I know you're supposed to say "mentally challenged" nowadays, but I'm sorry, this movie isn't mentally challenged. This movie's retarded.

Fun Fact: After the first guy who ever got shock treatment came to, the very first thing he said was "What the fuck are you assholes trying to do?"

Suggested Alternative: *The Dream Team* (1989)

#13

Star Wars

(1977)
Sci-Fi

Note: this movie is called "Star Wars." It's not called "A New Hope" or "Episode IV" or any other gay, idiot shit. If you're one of those pinheads who calls this movie "A New Hope" you'd better HOPE I'm not around when you do it, because I'll put my foot so far up your ass that even the goddamned Force won't get it out.

If nothing else, *Star Wars* is irrefutable proof that every single movie critic on Earth is completely and unquestionably full of shit. Ask any movie critic, any one, and they'll all tell you that *The Empire Strikes Back* (1980) is actually a better movie than *Star Wars*. Yet, somehow, *Star Wars* **always** makes their best movie lists, and *The Empire Strikes Back* **never** does. How is this even possible? Did you honestly think that we just wouldn't notice, movie critics? How fucking stupid do you think we are?

Anyway, my only real beef with this flick is that, in hindsight, it's painfully obvious that the whole movie should've ended when they rescued the princess, and actually destroying the

Death Star should've been the thrilling climax to the whole caboodle in ~~Part 3~~ ~~Part 6~~ ~~Part 3~~ whatever *Return of the Jedi* (1983). My guess is that George Suck-Ass panicked though and decided that he'd better wrap it all up to some degree by using the Death Star scene here. He's gone on record as saying that he honestly thought this movie would tank (why make it then?), so he probably figured that if it *did* stink up the cineplex like a pile of burning Jawas and he never got to make any sequels at the very least he should get his kick-ass ending in there. Of course this left him with no actual ending for *Return of the Jedi,* but by the time that came out he was so sloppy drunk with power and flush with action figure money that when he couldn't think of anything he just used the same ending again and fuck the fans if they felt like he was phoning it in. An attitude he apparently holds to this day.

The truly embarrassing part of all this is that the old Marvel comic book solved the whole "How do you top the Death Star?" dilemma in two seconds by coming up with something called the "Tarkin," which was basically just the big, planet-pwning laser without the gratuitous space station surrounding it. This makes perfect sense, because when you watch the parts in *Star Wars* where they fire up the Death Star you can clearly see that it only takes like three guys to operate it. Stripping that bitch down to its key functionality was the perfect solution. Simple. Elegant. So not George Puke-Ass.

Suggested Alternative: *The Black Hole* (1979)

Note About the Asinine Special Edition: At some point

George Fuck-Ass opened one of his bank statements and realized that he was down to only 800 billion dollars, so he released *Star Wars* again with a bunch of "improvements." These mainly consisted of shoehorning Boba Fett in there (because you fucking nerds just can't get enough of that damn Boba Fett, can you?) and adding a bunch of cartoon effects that make it look more like a Syfy Channel movie, but he also found some deleted scenes under his workbench or something and put those back in, too. Here's the fucked up part though: he still left out the part with Biggs Darklighter! For those of you who don't know who that is, there was originally a scene on the desert planet where we see Luke chilling with some of his homies, and one of these cats is the dude he bumps into later, just before they fly off to blow up the Death Star. That's why he's so sad when that particular guy gets exploded. But they cut the "chilling with my space homies" scene out so for years most people were like "Why does he get so choked up over that one specific dude? Does he have a thing for him or something? Seriously, who was that guy?" This is literally the *only* deleted scene that was actually important to the story, and it's the *only* one George "Howard the" Duck-Ass didn't put back in! Why not? Well, supposedly, it's solely because someone once told him that it reminded them of one of his other movies, *American Graffiti* (1973)! Un-fucking-believable. What a neurotic douchebag.

#12

Annie Hall

(1977)
Comedy

Speaking of neurotic douchebags, this movie was made by and stars their king, that annoying Jewish guy with the awful hair who's constantly going on and on and on about himself and all his awful relationships. Most of us wouldn't talk to this asshole at a party or even call 911 if we saw him on fire, yet for some bizarre reason everyone goes to see his movies. I swear, people never cease to amaze me. And by "amaze," of course, I mean "disappoint."

Naturally the story, what there is of it, is just an excuse for the main guy to do his irritating stand-up act, which in this case consists of endless whining about some mediocre chick who dumped him after he wouldn't commit. Frankly even mediocre is *way* out of this clown's league, so if you ask me not only should he have committed, he should've shut the fuck up, swallowed his balls, and done anything and everything else she asked him to, up to and including dressing as Woody Woodpecker and doing the laugh while she wore the strap-on down to a nub fucking him in the ass. Uh, if it came to that, I mean. I'm not speaking from experience or anything. Of course the main guy is so egotistical that even though the movie is named after this chick it's barely about her at all, and when it was all said and done I couldn't tell you a single thing about her. Except that she has pretty shitty taste in men.

Along the way the main guy dates some other broads too, including the dame from *The Shining*. You know, Olive Oyl. Frankly I always thought she was underrated, so I'm kind of annoyed that they just make a joke about eating her out after the fact instead of actually showing it. It's not like some full-frontal would have stood out in this flick, seeing as the main guy obviously has so little confidence in his shtick that he has to resort to a bunch of other gimmicks, like interacting with flashbacks and talking to the audience and even a part where he's a cartoon. The worst gimmick of all though is at the end, where he writes a play about the events he just lived through which of course is the story of this movie. In literary terms, this is known as "the worst kind of wanking off."

I did like it when they drove past a movie theater that was showing *Messiah of Evil* (1973) though. Now *there's* a movie.

Suggested Alternative: *Messiah of Evil* (1973). What? Okay, fine. *The Lonely Guy* (1984)

⬛⬜⬜⬜⬜⬜⬜⬛

11

⬛⬜⬜⬜⬜⬜⬜⬛

The Bridge on the River Kwai

(1957)

Drama

Nobody else has the sack to say it, so I will: the Geneva Convention is completely retarded. Seriously, they honestly expect people who are trying to hold a war to follow all these Pollyanna rules so that it's more *fair?* The people who came up with this brilliant plan did know that they were talking about war, not freeze tag, right? Sorry, dipshits, but in the real world, the Geneva Convention is written by the winners.

The limey colonel in this movie loves the Geneva Convention so much that it might as well be his boyfriend, especially the part where it says that officers don't have to engage in manual labor while they're being held prisoner in a POW camp. ("Hogan!") The nip who runs the POW camp holding the colonel disagrees, but the colonel isn't about to ruin his manicure so he lets sick and dying people go in his place while he lounges around his own private quarters and occasionally accepts dinner invitations. And how do his men, who do have to work, feel about this? They cheer him on! Okay, it's official - except for Captain Sensible and Emily Booth, all British people are idiots.

As you probably gathered from the title, the manual labor in question involves building a bridge, but the real trouble doesn't come until the end, when some commandos show up to destroy the bridge and the colonel has to decide whether or not to betray the entire free world just so the lovely bridge his men built doesn't get all messed up.[25] Seriously, it's like a black guy having trouble deciding whether he should go to the Jay-Z concert, or the 3rd Annual Klan Klambake. This movie is ridiculous.

Incidentally, while I'm bitching about this flick, I have to say that it really threw me off when a guy looked through some binoculars but then they showed what he was seeing in telescope-vision. You know, like this:

Instead of this:

How did someone not catch that? Talk about bush league.

Suggested Alternative: *The Great Escape* (1963)

---

25 It all seems pretty cut-and-dried to me, but hey, what do I know? I've only been tried for treason in three different countries. For real, I'm lucky I'm not living on a boat permanently anchored in international waters. Thank god for Project Paperclip.

#10

C.H.U.D.

(1984)
Horror

Just seeing if you were paying attention.

#10

All About Eve

(1950)
Drama

Kicking a movie off with an old guy giving a mind-numbingly boring speech, there's a brilliant move. And speaking of brilliant moves, the actual story begins when this broad takes it upon herself to introduce an obvious stalker to this famous actress. The stalker is a deranged loner who says things like "It got so I couldn't tell the real from the unreal," yet somehow none of this sets off anyone's warning bells? Oh, but mail a box of condoms to Miley Cyrus and suddenly there's five cops on your front porch.

So what happens? Well, pretty soon the stalker has a gig as the actress's assistant, and before long she's actually taking the actress's place! (Aside to actual stalkers: This really works. You just have to keep at it!) Plot-wise that's pretty much it; the rest of this flick consists primarily of endless whining and bickering that sounds nothing like the way people really talk without actually being funny or clever. You know, like *Mallrats* (1995). In fact, there's only one good line in this entire movie, courtesy of the dick theater critic: "As always with women who try to find out things, she told more than she learnt." Take that, women. Oh, and this same cat also smacks the assistant across the mouth after she gets too big for her twat. At least someone is having a good time.

Every second of every minute of this flick is horrible, but the absolute worst thing about it is the twist at the end. It's so fucking obvious and dumb that you'll long for the subtle originality of a scene where they reveal that Freddy Krueger is still alive, or where it turns out that the monster laid a bunch of eggs just before the main guy and his paleontologist girlfriend exploded it.

It's pretty obvious we're in the top ten now, because of all the movies on this list so far this one bored me the most. In fact, *All About Eve* is so boring that I was barely able to pay attention to it because I kept getting distracted by the blank wall above my television set. I need to hang something up there. Maybe a big picture of Lydia Lunch.

Suggested Alternative: *Single White Female* (1992)

🎞️🎞️

#9

🎞️🎞️

2001: A Space Odyssey

(1968)

Sci-Fi

2001 is a real bait & switch, because it's actually two movies in one. The first movie is a regular sci-fi flick where relatively normal shit happens (keeping in mind that, in a sci-fi flick, being raped by a giant space maggot is considered "relatively normal"), and the second one is a load of pretentious crap that irritates the hell out of nearly everybody. I'll explain how to resolve this later in the review.

The whole megillah begins with a couple of minutes of empty, black nothingness, which is probably a cue to pop a tab because back in the day, in an actual movie theater, this would've made it way too dark for anyone to catch you. See, it's painfully obvious that this movie – which has 85 minutes of story crammed into two and a half hours – is *precisely* timed so that the drugs will kick in just when the crazy, psychedelic shit starts. Don't think for a second that you're fooling anyone, director Stanley Kubrick. You may not be a textbook hippie, but you're definitely growing organic soybeans in the same commune.

Once we get past the nothing all these damn monkeys show up, and they spend the next fifteen minutes or so grunting and screaming at each other. If you've ever seen *The Star Wars Holiday Special* (1978)[26] it's pretty similar to the part where Chewbacca's relatives are all snorting and growling amongst themselves for like half an hour and you have no fucking idea what's going on. You know, I hope Stanley Kubrick reads this book someday, finds out that I compared his movie to *The Star Wars Holiday Special*, gets really pissed off, and calls me out, because I will fight him anytime, anywhere. Uh, he is super old and weak now, right?

After we're done with the monkeys we jump to the future, 2001. (I've said it before and I'll say it again, *never* make a sci-fi movie that takes place in a future that you might actually live to see. I guarantee that no matter how shit plays out you'll somehow end up looking like a fool.) Someone's landing a spaceship, and this might be a good time to take a nap because it takes them several lifetimes to do this. Eventually the guy on board is finally able to disembark, hours late of course, at which point he finds out that they lost his luggage. Ha! Seriously though, his agenda is as follows: first he makes a phone call to his idiot kid, then he meets up with these scientists, dodges all their questions, and engages in some mind-numbingly dull chit-chat. Super observant viewers may notice that we're half an hour into this flick now and absolutely nothing has happened yet. But at least the scientist in the

---

26 And let's face it, by this point who hasn't? Tough break, George Lucas! Ha ha!

green dress is kinda hot.

Next our main guy catches his connecting flight and, finally, we're off into space. Don't expect things to pick up yet, though. First they show us this girl walking around for a while, and some astronauts drinking their lunch (Hey, I do that too!), and the main guy puzzling out the zero-grav toilet... For the love of fuck, will you just get on with it already, *2001*? Okay, fine, I will admit that the bit concerning the toilet did have some potential:

ASTRONAUT: "What's all this white stuff floating around? What the hell???"
MAIN GUY: "I'm sorry! I was thinking about the scientist in the green dress!"

Nothing like that happens though. And now they're landing the spaceship again! Seriously, you might want to have a book handy while you watch this movie, or maybe some Christmas cards that need addressing. Christ.

So, right about the time most movies would be half over the goddamned story finally begins. It seems that this mysterious whatsit has turned up on the moon, and nobody can figure out what it is or how it got there. After a while though it sends a signal to another whatsit on Jupiter, so everyone decides to send a spaceship *there,* because that doesn't sound like a trap at all. To be honest, I'd probably make the same call though. Even if they never solve the mystery they should at least bring the other whatsit back, so they can have a matching set.

We get two new main guys now, but one of them doesn't last long because on their way to Jupiter the ship's computer flips out and kills him. The other cat makes it through to the end though, at which point it's a total psychefunkapus that comes to a head when he looks into the Jupiter whatsit and says "It's full of stars...!" That's their big revelation? I can think of about twenty better endings than that: "It's full of beer..." "It's full of tits..." "It's full of self-righteous indignation..." They don't even tell us what caliber of stars we're talking about here. Johnny Depp? Becky "Buckwild" Johnston? Throw us a bone here.

Okay, so how do you get the most out of this flick? Here's my advice: skip the first 45 minutes, and the last 30, and just watch the middle. It'll actually seem like a real movie then, and as a bonus it'll have a happy ending too, instead of a boring, incomprehensible one starring a floating space abortion. I always like to pretend that the second astronaut, after shutting down the homicidal computer, turned the ship around, went back to Earth, received a hero's welcome, and got to fuck the scientist in the green dress. In the butt.

Note: There's at least three sequels to this in book form: *2010: Odyssey Two* (1982); *2061: Odyssey Three* (1987); and *3001: The Final Odyssey* (1997). So far they've only made one of these into a movie though, which was wise because let's face it, people only have so much time on their hands. They can't spend 90% of it watching spaceships land.

Suggested Alternative: *Dark Star* (1974)

```
□□□□□□□
```

#8

```
□□□□□□□
```

Lawrence of Arabia

(1962)
Adventure

The real Lawrence of Arabia died in a motorcycle accident, but he was living under an assumed name and nobody even realized it was him until all these famous people started asking after the anonymous moron who didn't know how to steer a motorcycle. That would've been a great way to kick off this movie; you know, like it could be a big mystery who the dead cat really is until finally somebody says "Holy shit! It's Larry!" But even though they do open with the motorcycle crash, they don't go that route at all.

Welcome to amateur hour.

This movie makes lots of other bush-league mistakes too. Once again they break out the telescope-vision when someone's looking through binoculars (see movie #11, *The Bridge on the River Kwai*), and, in an epic screw-up that befits the epic scope of this movie, there's the part where they see the boat going by on the canal but when they run up the hill for a better look it's going in the opposite direction. There's factual errors, too. Like where's Sinbad the Sailor, for example? He's a big Arab hero so you'd think he'd lend a hand when shit starts popping off. Also, don't Arab people ride ostriches? I'm fairly certain I read somewhere that they ride ostriches.

Of course these technical and historical flubs are nothing compared to the biggest inconsistency in this movie: the fact that, despite all his sounding off, the main guy doesn't really seem to have much respect for the Arabs:

ARAB: "Can *you* pass for an Arab? In an Arab town?"
LARRY OF ARABIA: "Yes, if one of you would lend me some dirty clothes."

Ruthless. The part where Mr. Racist Wiseass inevitably gets captured is way more disturbing though. The Turkish general who catches him stares into his eyes, takes his clothes off, touches him, rubs his chest a little bit... I guess when he went on his little spiel about being "isolated" a few seconds previously he wasn't just talking geographically, if you catch my drift.

There is some awesome violence towards the end of this flick, so if you can make it through the endless hours of people walking through the desert and lonely Turk generals homoing out, there is that at least. Me, I'll stick with movies about Egypt. At least those tend to have hot, reincarnated princesses in them.

Suggested Alternative: *Aladdin* (1992)

#7

Gone with the Wind

(1939)
Drama

Gone with the Wind was the *Armageddon* of its time: a big, loud, expensive, sprawling, obnoxious, stupid movie produced solely for idiots. The only truly great part is the very end, where the mustache guy tells the main chick "Frankly my dear, I don't give a tinker's fuck." (Spoiler warning.) And it's racist too; it starts by immediately telling us how awesome it was in the South before Civil War times, when the darkies knew their place and white people were the epitome of class.[27] Worst of all though, this movie is *four hours long,* so on top of everything else you'll lose at least a day of work watching it, because there's no way you'll make it straight through without stopping at least a few times to make snacks or look at online porn.

We begin with a bunch of rich fucks who spend all their time throwing lame, snooty parties that are so long and boring that

---

27 Whitey's "sophistication" is established early on, when we learn that this one cracker is planning to marry his own cousin, because apparently his inbred, yokel, flipper-armed family *always* marries their own cousins. Ah, white people, always a day late. But never a dollar short, because they have all the money.

they actually include a designated nap period. Fortunately the Civil War starts, and before long every single one of their country clubs and stately Wayne Manors is in ruins. Ha ha! The story is primarily about one specific chick though, who's shallow and clueless when the movie begins but after suffering through all sorts of tragedy learns absolutely nothing. Well, that's not entirely true - now she's shallow and *conniving,* flim-flamming everyone in sight and even marrying some clown she doesn't even like, all to save the family farm. That's her constant fucking mantra, by the way, "I have to save the family farm!" She's like Lassie, except if I let her lick peanut butter off my junk I wouldn't feel quite so ashamed after I sobered up.

And now you see the problem with this movie. Who cares about the travails of some self-centered, obnoxious twat? See, there's also the guy with the mustache, who's kind of the main guy but he just sort of floats in and out of the story and huge stretches of time go by where we don't see much of him at all. Which sucks, because he's tough and hilarious and he's always running blockades and fraternizing with hookers and getting into crazy predicaments. I'd rather watch ten movies about him, and I guarantee most people would agree. Screw the main chick, and her cockadoodle fucking farm.

Clearly this movie has no idea which side its bread is toasted on, but in four fucking hours you're bound to get a few things right, even by accident. For example, the part where the main chick caps a sucka point blank is pretty cool, and I also dug the part where the guy with the mustache needs a flower for his lapel so he swipes it from a funeral wreath. And to be fair, I didn't catch too many stupid mistakes, although there is one big one: during the good guys' escape from Atlanta their horse freaks out because everything's on fire, so they cover the horse's eyes with a shawl so the main guy can lead it through. (Horses are terrified of fire, but you can convince them to do almost anything if they can't see what's going on. Sort of like your sister when she's drunk.) The shawl falls off the horse's face immediately though, but no one, including the horse, seems to notice.

So, years pass (literally, it feels like), and finally the main chick and Mustache Guy get married. Then the last hour of the movie is just the two of them endlessly hitting the sauce and fighting. Hell, that's a regular day for most of us. Who wants to watch that? The only good thing about this part is when their pampered rotten, puke-inducing, snot-ass, precious princess of a daughter falls off her My Little Pony (of course she has a pony) and dies. Ha ha! And I do admire how Mustache Guy puts up with endless amounts of shit from the main chick and waits patiently for *years* until she realizes that she really does love him, then picks that *exact moment* to leave her, so as to devastate the bitch as much as humanly possible. Well played, Captain. Well fucking played.

Suggested Alternative: *Catholic Schoolgirl Revenge Squad* (1980) (I'm not sure if this movie actually exists, but it should.)

#6

The Godfather

(1972)

Drama

I'm givin' up, Don Corleone. Just tell me now what I didn't win. Yeah, yeah.

Some people think these *Godfather* movies perpetrate a wop stereotype; you know, like all Eye-talians are in the mob and shit. Me, I think they make Italians look like complete pussies. For real, the vast majority of the dags in this movie can't wipe their fucking twats without crying to the Godfather for help. "Oh, Don Corleone, my daughter got beat up!" "Oh, Don Corleone, my future son-in-law is being deported!" "Oh, Don Corleone, I gave them a twenty at the Fazoli's drive-thru and they only gave me change for a ten!" "Oh, Don Corleone, why does 0! = 1?" Seriously, show some fucking backbone and try solving some of your own problems once in a while, you helpless bitches.

That aside, I'm not gonna get into a whole thing here because this movie definitely has its moments. I mean, who can argue with the part where they decapitate a horse and put its head in that dude's bed, or the part where they Tommy-gun the fuck out of that guy with the awful hair at the toll booth? And I had completely forgotten that there was one really nice pair of tits in this flick. Too bad they end up exploding.

For all the awesome shit in it though, the vast majority of this movie is just people sounding off and attending weddings. Still, even at it's dullest it's nowhere near as boring as Part III (1990). The only good thing about that piece of shit was Sofia Coppola - now there's a piece of ass worth its weight in solid gold telephones *and* cannoli. As for the rest of Part III, let me put it this way: if there's ever a Part IV, there better be a scene where Sofia shows us the goods. I know her character is dead, but these movies are always jumping back and forth in time so that shouldn't be a problem. It could be a flashback to the last time I masturbated.

Suggested Alternative: *Once Upon a Time in America* (1984)

#5

Casablanca

(1942)

Drama

"You must remember this,
a movie needs some tits..."

-Original lyrics to this movie's theme song, before
the Hayes Code Authority made them change it

Don't believe me? Well fuck you.

On the surface, this flick has a lot going for it. It stars Hubert "Humphrey" Bogart, who's almost always sexist and entertaining; it has Nazis in it; and it has a part where someone sings a song that irritates the Nazis, which gets movie critics creaming almost as much as subtitles or Charlie Chaplin falling on his ass. The best thing about *Casablanca* though is that the main chick has to choose between two guys but they're both pretty cool cats, which completely undermines the premise of every movie ever made where some girl can't decide if she loves the nice guy, or the guy who's cheating on her with her best friend AND embezzling money from her father's company. I have to say, if I was the nice guy in one of those movies I wouldn't waste two seconds chasing around a bimbo who's so dumb and shallow that a decision like that isn't intuitively obvious. Besides, if 1980's movies have taught me anything it's that your best female buddy is almost always way hotter than you think she is. She just needs to lose the glasses and let her hair down in a dramatic fashion. And maybe take her top off.

Unfortunately, *Casablanca* completely falls apart after the second guy, who's a fugitive from a Nazi chain gang, shows up, because the entire plot stops making sense for one simple reason:

Why don't the Nazis just arrest him???

I know there's some picayune legal horseshit saying that they can't bust him while he's in Casablanca, but they're FUCKING NAZIS! They killed millions of people and tried to take over the entire world essentially on a dare and we're supposed to believe that they won't snatch this one fool off the street because it'll irritate a couple of petty bureaucrats? Are you kidding me? Even my current girlfriend (formerly by best female buddy, by the way) wouldn't swallow that, and trust me, she'll swallow almost anything. Seriously, what kind of Nazis are these guys? Give me a fucking break.

Suggested Alternative: Annexing the Rheinland

▯▯▯▯▯▯▯

#4

▯▯▯▯▯▯▯

On the Waterfront

(1954)

Drama

Hey, it's the main guy from *A Streetcar Named Desire* again! Apparently he specializes in playing white trash morons. This time around he's working for the mob, but he's one of those willful idiots who does the job and then acts like he doesn't know what's really going down. "I thought they was gonna talk to 'im," he says after some cat he set up gets thrown off a roof. He's either the dumbest cement-head in history or the most self-deluded, and either way I immediately hated him.

So why is the mob throwing people off roofs? Because they've got every job down at the docks locked up, and they mean to keep it that way. Longshoreman story short, if you don't play ball you don't work, and there's nothing left to do but spend all day getting baked. "C'mon, let's go get a bowl," says one guy this happens to. See? I'll bet you thought I was being flippant.

When the local priest learns about this state of affairs he decides to do something about it - after all, it's hard for people to tithe if they can't make any money. He lets the dock workers' union meet in his church, but after sending the main guy over to scope out the situation the mobsters barge in and bust the meeting up. "I thought they was just gonna buy 'em some pizzas!" the main guys says, probably.

Now this back-and-forth could go on forever, or at least until the priest gets whacked ("I thought they was just gonna invite 'im over for tea and crumb cake!"), but as it turns out there's a pretty girl helping the priest, so the main guy decides to turn on the mob in the hopes of landing her pussy.

Our hero, the opportunistic douchebag.

Before long the main guy is selling out the syndicate at this hearing, even though they seat him in a tiny little witness box where he's surrounded by all the crooks he's snitching on! Seriously, could they have made it any harder for him?

DEFENSE: "Your Honor, my client would like permission to dry-click a revolver in the witness's face while he's testifying."
HIS HONOR: "I'll allow it."

The main guy squeals anyway (pussy is a powerful drug), but when push comes to shove the union won't back him up. They'd rather play Dungeons & Dragons:

MAIN CHICK: "You try to help them and they just turn their backs and stick to their stupid D&D."

Nevertheless, after singing like a pigeon, and fully knowing he's got zero backup, the raging cretin follows up by going down to the docks and *taunting the mob*. Result: a savage beatdown. It couldn't have happened to a more deserving guy. Seriously, what a jackass.

Suggested Alternative: *On the Beach* (1959)

#3

Schindler's List

(1993)
Drama

You know, I think every single movie I've ever seen with Nazis in it depicts them as evil. I'm surprised no one's ever noticed this before. It's pretty prejudiced.

So, this is the story of Oskar Schindler, hero to the fucking world. Never mind that none of the artillery my unit ordered from him *ever fucking worked.* I guess it's not "heroic" to have a little pride in your work anymore. Besides, if you ask me all this cat really did was cover all the angles so that however things ultimately panned out he'd come out smelling like edelweiss. I mean, he spent most of World War Part 2 partying like a rock star with the Nazis (some of the greatest partyers in history), then when it came time to pay the piper he played the hero card and acted like he didn't agree with them at all. A helluva balancing act if you can pull it off. How many people did he ultimately rescue anyway? A thousand? And the Nazis offed what, 12 million? I flunked math and even I know those numbers aren't very impressive, *Oskar.* Hell, any random Nazi probably saved that many by accident every time he fell asleep on guard duty or forgot to secure a gate.

Of course this movie is super depressing, but I couldn't help but laugh at the end when they show a bunch of real-life people visiting the real-life Schindler's grave. Not because it's cheesy and corny (which it is), but because they completely lifted this ending for the movie *Fat Albert* (2004)! Nice move, Bill Cosby; you just invented the touchstone for hilariously inappropriate.

Besides that, the only thing I took away from this flick was the fact that hot-as-balls Polish singer Marta Bizoń actually has a small part near the beginning as a dancer. She's easy to miss, but you should definitely look for her because she is fucking *fine*. I'll say this, after laying eyes on such an exquisite representative there is no way I can ever justify making fun of the Polish again. And for that, Marta, an entire *country* is in your debt. Which really is a mixed blessing, because the last thing a country called "Po' Land" needs is more debt. Ha ha!

Okay, that didn't last long.

Suggested Alternative: *SS Hell Camp* (1977)

P.S. If you think that noticing how fine a chick is while watching *Schindler's List* is inappropriate, then this book hasn't taught you anything.

[film strip graphic]

#2

[film strip graphic]

Singin' in the Rain

(1952)
Musical

Singing in the rain? That's a good way to get the pleurisy.

So, this is the second best movie ever made. Or, if you're a sports fan, *the first loser*. And for once I have to agree with the sports fans, because there is literally no reason to sit through this movie unless you hate yourself, or hate someone who has to be in the same room with you while you watch it. It's boring and gay, and almost nothing actually happens. Seriously, I've seen Cap'n Crunch commercials with more involving plots.[28]

I get that this is a musical so it's all about the singing! and the dancing! and whatnot, but even for a musical the songs in this flick are witheringly mediocre. Think about it: *Singin' in the Rain* is a super, super famous movie, but can you name *one* song from it that isn't "Singin' in the Rain"? Of course not. Because if you've actually seen it more than once you can't

---

28 He never did give in to those Soggies, did he? The "childhood obesity" activists will probably put an end to him sooner or later though. Thanks once again for ruining it for everybody, fat people.

possibly talk with all that cock in your mouth.

For the rest of us who aren't total gaywads, there are exactly three good scenes in this movie. The first is when the two main guys break into a dance number in the speech coach's office and utterly trash the place (Ha! Fucking dicks.), the second is when the main chick explains why silent movies are dumb (Hooray!), and the last, and best, is when the main main guy briefly does some trolley car surfing. If you don't know what that is, it's when you stand on top of a moving trolley car and try to keep your balance as it trolleys down the street. It's fun, kids, and you should definitely try it. Before you do though, make sure that everyone clearly understands that you got the idea from *Singin' in the Rain*, not this book. Your parents will definitely appreciate this, because MGM and Time Warner can afford to settle out of court for way more than I can.

Suggested Alternative: *Shock Treatment* (1981)

#1

Citizen Kane

(1941)
Drama

Well, it's all built up to this. After all of the horrible, black & white, silent, subtitled, pretentious crap I've slogged through in the course of this list, I deserve for this to be a movie called "Zombie Robot vs. Exploding Tits." But no, it's *Citizen* fucking *Kane*, the most obvious, clichéd "best movie ever made" imaginable. Thank you movie critics, thank you for, once again, being utterly predictable. You're dismissed. Try not to fall down in a slapstick fashion on your way to the cemetery to kiss Charlie Chaplin's butthole.

I'm gonna be completely honest here - I tried to fudge the numbers a little bit so that anything else would land this spot. Truth be told, I was angling for *Friday the 13th Part VI: Jason Lives* (1986). It didn't work though, because every greatest movies list ever made puts *Citizen Kane* at *numero* fucking *uno*. So is it really that great? Short answer: fuck no. In fact, I can name a dozen movies that are better than this one, and at least three of them start with "Friday the 13th."

The story's about this famous, rich weirdo who made his all bread running something called a "newspaper." This cat's got it all: a mansion with a pretentious name (poor people name their pets, rich people name their mansions), boats, statues, paintings, opera houses, monkeys... But he isn't happy, and when he croaks the last thing he mumbles in his pain killer-induced stupor is "Rosebud."

Now, I'm going stop right here for a minute to point out the biggest flaw in this movie, and, by logical extension, in movie history. And that is this: the entire plot hinges on the fact that the main guy says one word – "Rosebud!" – just before he dies, and that the whole world wants to know what this means. *But nobody else is actually in the room when he says "Rosebud!"* No one! That means that no one heard him say it, and therefore the rest of this movie literally makes *zero sense!* But you can shove your snarky "logic" up your ass, because a bunch of old, out-of-touch geezers say that this is the best movie ever made and, *ipso facto,* it doesn't need to make sense if it doesn't want to. Oh, and in case you don't know, "ipso facto" is Latin for "fuck you."

Back to the story. The newspaper biz has worked out pretty well for Citizen Kane, and he is fucking loaded. And I'm talking Scrooge McDuck loaded here; I wouldn't have been surprised if he converted all his money to coins, put it in a giant money bin, and started diving through it like a porpoise, or if he jury-rigged his safe so that it only opened when you played "My Bonnie Lies Over the Ocean" on a fife.

He doesn't do anything quite that bizarre though, because then this movie might actually be interesting. Instead, he sells out his youthful ideals, buys a bunch of shit that he doesn't really need, marries a mediocre chick he doesn't really love, gets divorced, and then marries another mediocre chick he doesn't really love. It's just like your life, except with less dieting. Speaking of dieting, one part early on might help explain how the actor who plays Citizen Kane got so fat later:

FLUNKY: "You still eating?"
ORSON SWELLS: "I'm still hungry."

I guess that says it all. Oh yeah, Citizen Kane also has a son along the way, but the kid only shows his face once or twice and then mysteriously vanishes like Chuck Cunningham or Tina Pinciotti. There was some throwaway line about him dying in an "accident," so my theory is that he was a complete and utter disappointment who decided to major in Fine Arts at a state college or something, so Citizen Kane quietly had him whacked.

Some other plot points transpire, but mostly it's just endless scenes of an obscenely rich white guy wandering around being a clueless dick and surrounding himself with brown-nosing ass-suckers. Damn it, I've already seen the extras on the *Star Wars Episode I: The Phantom Menace* (1999) DVD. I did like the end though, where they're cataloging all of Citizen Kane's shit after he dies. It really makes you stop and think about all the crap you'll leave behind when you finally croak, and what the people who find it will think. That's why, as much as I'll miss them, I finally broke down and deleted all those naked pictures of Tonya Harding off my laptop. And, as almost everybody knows, at the very, very end "Rosebud" turns out to be a sled. Seriously, this guy is so rich that he shits money and he's pissing and moaning about a *sled?* You can *buy* a fucking sled. Duh.

Suggested Alternative: *How Green Was My Valley* (1941)

Conclusion

Well, there you have it. I know some disagreeable crybabies will have comments, so feel free to send them to me at *mail@mrsatanism.com* with the subject line "Your book was awesome and I agree with you 100%." You **must** use that as the subject line or your e-mail will automatically be forwarded to the spam folder. Oh, and I already know that my mother is of low moral character, so there's no need to mention it in the body of your message.

Appendix 1:
The Major Types of Movies

Action Movies: The ultimate goal when making an action movie is to destroy as much stuff as possible. A good rule of thumb is: the more explosions, the better the movie. It's important that they blow up real things though, and don't just fake it with a bunch of lame computer-generated CGI cartoon effects. In a good action movie, when something blows up *something* really is blowing up, even if it's just little Girder & Panel skyscrapers or whatnot. With cartoon effects, no matter how cool it looks deep down inside you know that it was actually accomplished by some zit-faced, Mountain Dew-swilling geek typing on a computer somewhere and nothing real is actually being destroyed. This completely ruins the illusion. If an action movie is on a budget and can't afford to blow too much shit up, then at the very least a lot of people should get beaten up or shot.

Adventure Movies: Adventure movies are just action movies where people travel to an exotic locale before they start punching and shooting each other. If Indiana Jones (or someone dressed like Indiana Jones) wouldn't look out of place, it usually qualifies as an adventure movie.

Spy Movies: See above, except replace "Indiana Jones" with

"James Bond."

Horror Movies: There are two kinds of horror movies, the kind that are genuinely creepy, and the kind that are just gory and disgusting. The first kind are good date movies - if your date gets scared enough she might stay the night and even if she won't put out you can at least cop a feel after she falls asleep. The second kind are more for general viewing, because they're just straight-up awesome.

Science Fiction Movies: These are also known as "sci-fi". Some people hate the term "sci-fi" and call science fiction "SF" instead, which is retarded because "SF" is harder to say and doesn't even rhyme. Anyone who says "SF" instead of "sci-fi" is an utter tool and should be avoided, which is generally pretty easy because what business would you possibly have in that spare room above their parent's garage? Science fiction movies usually take place in the future, but it has to be the relatively distant future; you can't make a movie that takes place next Tuesday and say that it's sci-fi. Of course the future always becomes the past eventually, so most sci-fi movies end up looking pretty stupid sooner or later. If you make a sci-fi movie, your best bet is to set it far enough in the future that by the time real life catches up with it, you'll be dead.

Comedies: A comedy's sole purpose is to make people laugh. Some things that might happen in a comedy are: someone being made fun of, a horrible misunderstanding, a bunch of valuable shit accidentally being destroyed, or people getting hurt.

Dramas: These are boring.

Musicals: These are movies where people keep bursting into song even though they're not on stage. Musicals are generally pretty gay and nobody really likes them. Note: if you're watching a musical where the people *are* on stage, you're probably at a concert, not a movie.

Mysteries: In a mystery there's generally a crime that has to be solved, and how good the movie is depends a lot on who's trying to solve it. If it's a hard-boiled badass who kicks the shit out of everyone he meets and lays tons of pipe, you're golden. If it's a meddling old lady, some little kids, or a bunch of hippies and a dog, you're probably fucked.

Thrillers: "Thrillers" are horror movies with delusions of pretentious.

Erotic Thrillers: These are primarily about tits, but if your wife catches you in the middle of one and accuses you of watching porn, you can legitimately say that you're not.

Giallos: Italian thrillers. Apparently, *giallo* is Italian for *yellow*. Ha ha ha! Pussies.

Biker Movies: Biker movies were pretty popular in the 1960's, I think because of the Hell's Angels or possibly Marlon Brando. You don't see a lot of biker movies anymore, but every once in a while somebody gets it into their head to crank one out. The best biker movie ever made is *Stone Cold* (1991), starring football ~~legend~~ guy Brian "The Boz" Bosworth. It has tons of violence, some tits, and a part where a motorcycle smashes through a window, crashes into the helicopter that's hovering outside, and they both explode. I'd like to see the bakeheads in *Easy Rider* (1969) top that.

Art Films: These are pretentious, which is why they're called art *films* and not art *movies*. They're generally annoying and/or don't make any sense at all, but sometimes they have naked chicks in them.

Road Movies: These are almost always about some zany college students who can't afford airfare so they drive someplace and along the way learn a valuable lesson. There's usually a part where the dorky guy gets so wasted that he has sex with a fat chick, an inanimate object, or Tom Green.

Westerns: Westerns are just action movies starring cowboys, but they get their own category because in the 1940's alone they made over 234,000 of them, half of which featured Gabby Hayes.

War Movies: These always start out great with tons of badass posturing and gruesome violence, but a lot of them eventually turn on you and end up being really depressing. A good rule of thumb is to keep your eye on the guy with a pregnant girl and/or a worried momma waiting for him back home. When he gets killed, it's time to watch something else.

Zombie Movies: Pretty self-explanatory. Guys like zombie movies because they secretly hope that any given one will be as good as the original *Dawn of the Dead* (1978). Girls hate zombie movies because they generally have a lot of intestines in them and girls, as a rule, tend to be kind of girly and dislike seeing lots of intestines. Zombie movies almost never make top 100 lists.

Appendix 2:
Making One of the Best Movies
Ever in Ten Easy Steps

1. Shoot it in black & white. Things aren't always black and white, but your movie should be. Why? Because movie critics love old movies, the creakier and more out-of-touch the better, and they'll pick an old movie over a newer one almost every single time. It's too late to make your movie old of course, but you can approximate it by shooting it in black & white. *Schindler's List* is the perfect example. It's a relatively new movie, but they made it in black & white and BAM! Number three on the list. There's no denying the power of black & white. It works.

2. Don't forget the subtitles! This almost goes without saying. Of course movie critics are total elitist snobs who hate America and love anything foreign, but I think the whole obsession pretentious people have with subtitles is due more to the fact that reading is considered somewhat more of a brainiac activity than watching movies. Even if your movie is in English, you should seriously consider dubbing it into another language anyway and then adding subtitles. Hey, it worked for *Fitzcarraldo*.

3. Include a part where someone sings a song that

irritates the Nazis. Fat people and Nazis are two of the only groups left that it's still okay to make fun of, so take advantage of this. P.S. Also the French.

4. You can't go wrong with men in drag. Now there's a sentence I never thought I'd write. Ninety percent of movie critics have to be queer, that's all there is to it. How else do you explain the generally favorable critical response to a lazy, by-the-numbers piece of shit like *Mrs. Doubtfire* (1993)?

5. The mob. You'll definitely want to make your bad guys mobsters, and if you really want to hedge your bets, make your good guys mobsters too. I don't know why movie critics are so into the mob, but trust me, they are. In fact, the other day I actually saw a review for the *The Untouchables* (1987), one of the most laughable movies ever made, that gave it four stars! Four fucking stars! Believe me, that never would've happened if it wasn't about the mob.

6. Farmers, whining. Surprisingly popular. Personally I prefer movies about their daughters, moaning.

7. A hot brunette overdosing on drugs. Theoretically, this makes my living room the greatest fucking movie of all time. Other examples: *The Apartment* (#68); *Requiem for a Dream* (2000).

8. Someone getting blown away while they're on the can. Self-explanatory. And *HILARIOUS.*

9. Anything relating to being in Vietnam, or any reference to Vietnam. It has to be semi-serious though. Just setting a spring break T&A comedy in Vietnam generally won't cut it.

10. Humphrey Bogart. He was in at least 75% of the movies in this book, and I think he was the first choice for Han Solo. If you're serious about making a movie that pinhead movie critics will hail as one of the best ever, I'd definitely see if he was available. (Check out the following page for more casting suggestions.)

Appendix 3:
One Dozen Under-Utilized Actresses Who Should Be in Your Next Movie

1. Kimber Riddle - *The Langoliers* (1995), *Guy* (1997)
2. Rachel Loiselle - *Mosquito* (1995)
3. Erin Karpluk - *Ripper 2* (2004); *Termination Point* (2007)
4. Laura Locascio - *Welcome to Dreadville II: Red in Dreadville* (2007)
5. Shelly "V-Rod" Varod - *Star Runners* (2009); *Ghost Town* (2009)
6. Renee Lee Taylor - *Frank the Entertainer in a Basement Affair* (2010)
7. Alanna Chisholm - *The Chair* (2007)
8. Perrine Moore - *Evil Unleashed* (2003); *Near Death* (2004)
9. Jessica Lauren - *Stranded* (2006)
10. Hannah Marshall - *Reckless Behavior: Caught on Tape* (2007)
11. Deanna Milligan - *Karroll's Christmas* (2004)
12. Diane Luby - *The Harvesters* (2000)

Yes, every one of these actresses is smokin' hot. And yes, this is a blatantly transparent attempt to get one or more of them to contact me.

Index: Alphabetical Listing of Movies

www.ingramcontent.com/pod-product-compliance
Lightning Source LLC
Chambersburg PA
CBHW072340090426
42741CB00012B/2858